The Demand for Housing
in Racially Mixed Areas

PUBLICATIONS OF THE
COMMISSION ON RACE AND HOUSING

Where Shall We Live? Report of the Commission on Race and Housing

Residence and Race: Final and Comprehensive Report to the Commission on Race and Housing by DAVIS MC ENTIRE

The Demand for Housing in Racially Mixed Areas: A Study of the Nature of Neighborhood Change by CHESTER RAPKIN AND WILLIAM G. GRIGSBY

Privately Developed Interracial Housing: An Analysis of Experience by EUNICE AND GEORGE GRIER

Property Values and Race: Studies in Seven Cities by LUIGI LAURENTI

Studies in Housing and Minority Groups edited by NATHAN GLAZER AND DAVIS MC-ENTIRE

The Demand for

Housing

in Racially Mixed Areas

A Study of the Nature of Neighborhood Change

CHESTER RAPKIN and WILLIAM G. GRIGSBY
Institute for Urban Studies, University of Pennsylvania

SPECIAL RESEARCH REPORT TO THE
COMMISSION ON RACE AND HOUSING AND
THE PHILADELPHIA REDEVELOPMENT AUTHORITY

UNIVERSITY OF CALIFORNIA PRESS

BERKELEY AND LOS ANGELES 1960

UNIVERSITY OF CALIFORNIA PRESS
BERKELEY AND LOS ANGELES
CALIFORNIA
CAMBRIDGE UNIVERSITY PRESS
LONDON, ENGLAND
© 1960 BY
THE REGENTS OF THE UNIVERSITY OF CALIFORNIA
LIBRARY OF CONGRESS CATALOG CARD NUMBER: 60-10360
PRINTED IN THE UNITED STATES OF AMERICA

Foreword

The Demand for Housing in Racially Mixed Areas by Chester Rapkin and William G. Grigsby was prepared in the Institute for Urban Studies, University of Pennsylvania, at the request of the Commission on Race and Housing. It is one of a series of studies undertaken for the Commission in connection with a broad inquiry into housing problems involving racial and ethnic minority groups. It also forms part of a larger Philadelphia study sponsored by the Philadelphia Redevelopment Authority.

Where the members of racial and ethnic minorities should live —whether in segregated communities or dispersed through the general housing supply—is a social problem of large and growing importance in American cities. To inquire into this problem was the purpose of the Commission on Race and Housing, formed in 1955. The Commission is an independent, private citizens' group, not a part of any other organization. Its work was made possible by a grant of $305,000 from the Fund for the Republic. The Fund's participation was limited to financial assistance, and it is not in any way otherwise responsible for the studies carried out for the Commission or for its conclusions.

The following persons served on the Commission in their individual capacities and not as representing any organizations or groups:

GORDON W. ALLPORT
   Professor of Psychology, Harvard University, Cambridge, Massachusetts.

ELLIOTT V. BELL
   Chairman of the Executive Committee and Director, McGraw-Hill Publishing Company; Editor and Publisher, *Business Week,* New York.

LAIRD BELL
   Attorney: Bell, Boyd, Marshall and Lloyd, Chicago.

REVEREND JOHN J. CAVANAUGH, C.S.C.
   Director, University of Notre Dame Foundation, Notre Dame, Indiana.

HENRY DREYFUSS
   Industrial Designer, South Pasadena, California, and New York.

PETER GRIMM
   Chairman of the Board and Director, William A. White and Sons, New York.

COL. CAMPBELL C. JOHNSON
   Assistant to the Director, Selective Service System, Washington, D.C.

CHARLES S. JOHNSON
   President, Fisk University, Nashville, Tennessee. Deceased.

CHARLES KELLER, JR.
   President, Keller Construction Corporation, New Orleans, Louisiana.

CLARK KERR
   President, University of California, Berkeley.

PHILIP M. KLUTZNICK
   Chairman of the Board, American Community Builders, Inc., Park Forest, Illinois.

HENRY R. LUCE
   Editor-in-Chief, *Time, Life, Fortune, Architectural Forum, House and Home,* and *Sports Illustrated,* New York.

STANLEY MARCUS
   President, Neiman-Marcus, Dallas, Texas.

HAROLD C. MCCLELLAN
   President, Old Colony Paint and Chemical Company, Los Angeles. Resigned following appointment as Assistant Secretary of Commerce in 1955.

WARD MELVILLE
   President, Melville Shoe Corporation, New York.

Francis T. P. Plimpton
Attorney: Debevoise, Plimpton and McLean, New York.
R. Stewart Rauch, Jr.
President, The Philadelphia Saving Fund Society, Philadelphia.
Robert R. Taylor
Secretary and Executive Director, Illinois Federal Savings and
Loan Association, Chicago. Deceased.
John H. Wheeler
President, Mechanics and Farmers Bank, Durham, North
Carolina.
Earl B. Schwulst, Chairman
President and Chairman of the Board, The Bowery Savings
Bank, New York.

Professor Robert K. Merton of Columbia University, Professor
Stuart W. Cook of New York University, and Dr. Robert C.
Weaver, formerly State Rent Administrator of New York, served
as research advisors to the Commission.

The central focus of research undertaken for the Commission
was on the problem of inequality of housing opportunity con-
nected with racial or ethnic distinctions, with emphasis on the
situation of Negroes, Puerto Ricans, Mexican-Americans, and
Orientals. The research was national in scope and endeavored to
comprehend all major ramifications of a very complex problem—
its causes, impacts and consequences, and directions of change.
Some thirty special studies and research memoranda were prepared for the consideration of the Commission by the research
director, his assistants, and coöperating social scientists in a dozen
universities.

The Commission has previously published its own conclusions
and recommendations in *Where Shall We Live?* (University of
California Press, 1958). A comprehensive report of the findings of
the entire study is found in *Residence and Race*, by the research director. In addition, several of the particular inquiries
which are of wide interest have been published; the others are
available in the library of the University of California at
Berkeley.

The particular contribution of the study by Dr. Rapkin and

Dr. Grigsby is an analysis of the process of neighborhood racial change from the standpoint of the housing market, including conditions of supply, demand, price, financing, and related factors. This is a much-discussed subject, on which there are pronounced differences of opinion but very few objective, systematic studies. The research findings reported in the present volume, therefore, help to fill an important need for knowledge of market processes in racial transition neighborhoods. The specific areas studied are in Philadelphia, but the conditions in these areas are reproduced, with variations, in virtually every large city in the country. The study, therefore, has far more than local significance.

In authorizing publication of research reports, including this one by Dr. Rapkin and Dr. Grigsby, the Commission on Race and Housing believes that the research was conscientiously and competently carried out, in accordance with high scientific standards. However, the Commission assumes no responsibility for the accuracy of specific data in the various reports, nor does it necessarily endorse all of the interpretations and conclusions drawn by the authors. Persons desiring to know the position of the Commission are referred to its own report.

EARL B. SCHWULST, Chairman
Commission on Race and Housing

New York City

Preface

It is our hope that this volume will shed some light on what is undoubtedly the most perplexing and compelling domestic problem of America at mid-century—the effort to assure full citizenship rights for all members of our society. In essence this study is primarily an analysis of some of the major forces at work in racially mixed neighborhoods, but it also attempts to probe into the nature and ultimate outcome of the transition process. This problem has been of growing importance, particularly in the cities of the North, as the Negro population has increased, often faster than the white, and as large numbers of Negroes have acquired residences in previously all-white areas.

The analysis of racial change is approached from the point of view of the housing market—the mechanism through which transition occurs. The residential pattern, however, obviously has implications that go beyond questions of housing alone. Racial concentration of residences affects the composition of schools, churches, community centers, and other activities that are organized on a neighborhood basis. But perhaps more important is the fact that segregated peoples do not have the opportunity to experience neighborly contacts, share community facilities, and participate in the solution of common problems. It is these types of interactions that develop mutual understanding and provide the true path to an integrated community.

This study was originally undertaken as part of a larger housing-market analysis whose purpose was to evaluate the demand for dwelling units in the Eastwick redevelopment area in Philadelphia. The larger study was sponsored by the Philadelphia Redevelopment Authority and conducted by the Institute for Urban Studies of the University of Pennsylvania. Additional funds contributed by the Commission on Race and Housing enabled us to expand the scope of the work and provided an opportunity for a greater depth of analysis.

After redevelopment, the Eastwick area will be a city within a city with residences for approximately 50,000 people, complete community facilities, and industrial and commercial areas. Ultimately close to $200,000,000 of public and private investment will be required to complete the task. But aside from its size and cost, the Eastwick project is impressive because it constitutes the first large-scale effort to market single family homes without discrimination by reason of race, religion, or national origin.

It was felt that this stipulation required a special appraisal of the influence of mixed occupancy on the general levels of potential demand for dwellings in the redevelopment area. To discover the influence of this factor, investigation was undertaken of market situations in which mixed racial occupancy was present. These were found to be of two general types. The first consisted of privately financed housing developments which as a matter of policy, stated or tacit, were available from their inception to families regardless of race. A selected group of these developments located in Philadelphia and in New York City was studied solely to determine the possible influence of open occupancy on demand. The results of this inquiry are reported elsewhere in a document entitled "Market Experience and Occupancy Patterns in Interracial Housing Developments" by Chester Rapkin. A separate and more intensive report on a suburban subdivision, "Buyers of Interracial Housing: A Study of the Market for Concord Park Homes," was prepared by George and Eunice Grier.

The second major source of experience was to be found in established areas of the city in which Negro as well as white families have access to the housing supply. A group of these mixed areas was subjected to intensive scrutiny and the results of this investigation are presented in this volume.

It is hardly an exaggeration to say that this study was in its essence a community enterprise. Well over one hundred persons generously contributed their time, knowledge, and records. They included public officials and professional persons, citizens' groups, civic associations, educators, churchmen, social workers, as well as our own colleagues at the University of Pennsylvania. It is our sincere wish that we could acknowledge each person by name, but we fear that such a list would leave little room for the remainder of the volume. We do wish to take special note of a number of persons who made substantial and material contributions to our work. Let us hasten to add, however, that our sincere appreciation is extended uniformly to all those who participated in this study.

Among the persons and agencies that aided us were: David Wallace and Una Oberman of the Philadelphia Redevelopment Authority; George Schermer, Burton Gordin, and John McDermott of the Philadelphia Commission on Human Relations; Jane Reinheimer Motz of the American Friends Service Committee; William Rafsky, director, and Mead Smith Karras of the Office of the Development Coördinator of the City of Philadelphia; Dorothy S. Montgomery, director, and Elfrieda Hoeber of the Philadelphia Housing Association; Maurice B. Fagan, director, and Nathan Agran of the Philadelphia Fellowship Commission; John Teller, executive secretary of the Philadelphia Board of Realtors; Postmaster Raymond A. Thomas, John T. Fleming, and William Regli of the Philadelphia Post Office; James A. Donaghy, president, Keystone Branch 157 of the National Association of Letter Carriers; I. Maximilian Martin, Howard Stoertz, and Kay Briner. Robert Weaver, Louis Winnick, and Herbert Gans read the preliminary drafts and offered many valuable suggestions. Mrs. Motz and Mrs. Briner carried out field inquiries and collected most of the primary data for the study of racial transition in West Mount Airy and Mr. Stoertz, past chairman of the Church Community Relations Council of Pelham, furnished an account of the organization and activities of that group (Appendix A).

The following staff members and consultants participated in various phases of the study: George Moed assisted in the formulation of the study design, preparation of the questionnaire, selection of the study areas, supervision of the field interviews, and the drafting of Appendix C. Janet Scheff Reiner similarly participated in the selection of study areas, the questionnaire design, and the drafting of a number of sections of chapters i and iii. In addition, she conducted all of the interviews with informed persons and prepared a full written report of her findings which provided significant background material for several chapters of the report. Thomas Shea prepared the early drafts of Appendix A on West Mount Airy and also undertook some of the tabulation and analysis of the data on prices and financing for the Tasker and Strawberry Mansion study areas. Hilda Hertz Golden drafted the original questionnaire and undertook the preliminary analysis of the data on characteristics, attitudes, and awareness of the respondents. Morton Baratz aided in the study of the Mount Airy area and provided valuable suggestions after reading the preliminary report. Marketers Research, Inc., Ernest Jurkat, president, conducted the field interviews and aided in the racial identification of blocks in the study areas.

Jerome Kaufman and Jerome Koffler were research assistants for a portion of the study. Attilio Bergamasco prepared the maps and graphs. June Harvey of the Commission on Race and Housing staff prepared the index. Cynthia B. Boone acted as secretary and administrative assistant throughout the study, working through many difficult tasks with grace and ease. Marga Walter and Barbara Siegle performed vital secretarial services at the last stages prior to publication.

We also wish to express our appreciation for the coöperation of Dr. Davis McEntire, research director of the Commission on Race and Housing, whose aid made it possible to enlarge the scope of the original study design. Above all, our thanks go to Professor William L. C. Wheaton, director of the Institute for Urban Studies, for his unflagging interest, constant encouragement, and incisive comments.

Although this is an empirical and, we hope, objective study, it contains certain expressions on the larger issues that were subject to investigation. We wish it made explicit that these views are not necessarily held either by the Institute for Urban Studies or the Commission on Race and Housing.

CHESTER RAPKIN
WILLIAM G. GRIGSBY

Contents

Text Tables

Text Figures

Appendix Tables

Appendix Figure

I

Introduction

In recent years the American Negro has made important strides toward economic and social equality. Full integration in the armed services is being achieved and has been accompanied by occupational and employment gains, greater equality in the use of public accommodations, and wider Negro participation in public affairs. Most notable, perhaps, has been the desegregation of many public schools following the Supreme Court decision of May, 1954.

Free entrance into the housing market remains one of the last problems of significance for the nonwhite[1] sector of the population. Even here, however, change is discernible, for in the past decade several factors operating in concert have enabled Negroes to enter residential areas previously closed to them. Probably the most important of these has been the confirmation of Negro rights in various legislative enactments and judicial pronouncements, foremost of which was the 1948 Supreme Court decision which declared restrictive covenants in real estate deeds to be unenforceable. At the same time, there has been a rapid relative and absolute increase in Negro incomes which has resulted in the emergence of a growing nonwhite middle class with sufficient purchasing power to acquire housing accommodations of higher

[1] Although the term "nonwhite" includes Orientals and American Indians as well as Negroes, in Philadelphia "nonwhite" is virtually synonymous with "Negro." In the 1950 Census less than 3,000 of the city's 378,000 nonwhites were not Negro. In the text of this and succeeding chapters, therefore, "Negro" and "nonwhite" are used interchangeably. In all tabular presentations, however, the precise wording is retained.

quality. Had the Supreme Court decision of 1948 come ten years earlier, its initial impact would have been far less, for at that time relatively few Negroes could afford to buy homes in white areas.

The problem of financing, another major stumbling block to the prospective Negro home purchaser, was materially eased by the Veterans Administration mortgage-loan guaranty program introduced in 1945. The lending community has traditionally regarded Negroes as poor financial risks. Mortgagees have pointed to the fact that in times of economic crisis Negroes are often the first to be separated from their jobs. As a result of the attitude of lenders, Negroes have usually paid higher interest rates, made larger down payments, and have frequently been forced to resort to secondary financing. This differential treatment, which quite obviously has put potential Negro homeowners at a significant disadvantage, was reduced considerably by the VA mortgage program which was available to a large segment of the Negro community.

The events and trends of recent years, although enabling an increasing proportion of the nonwhite population to obtain a better living environment, have by no means eliminated all of the barriers which Negroes face in the housing market. A Negro veteran with a good, steady income can still be, and probably often is, refused a mortgage loan should he wish to purchase a house in an all-white area. Similarly, he may be discriminated against by the owner who has put up his home for sale. The seller, either because of his own fears about Negroes, or his fears about his neighbor's fears, may be very reluctant to be the first white person in his neighborhood to sell to a nonwhite. And finally, Negroes themselves, knowing the feelings of many whites, may understandably hesitate to pioneer their way into a new area.

Thus, the legal and economic power available to Negroes has been offset to some degree by formidable social obstacles. Nevertheless, in many northern cities the increasing market freedom which Negroes now enjoy, coupled with rapid growth in the nonwhite population, has resulted in the entrance of Negroes into white neighborhoods at an unprecedented rate. In many of these neighborhoods, Negro purchases have been confined to a few blocks, and as a result, there has been a rather quick transformation to sections with only a few whites in residence. In order neighborhoods, however, nonwhite in-migration has departed from the pattern of the past. Negro purchases have been widely dispersed throughout an area, and the sections they have entered have remained interracial in character for a number of years.

The number of racially changing areas in various northern and western cities has now become quite large. Moreover, Negro entry into many neighborhoods which are presently all white is a certainty. The expansion process has become a matter of both hope and serious concern to large sectors of the population. Despite this fact, there is very little knowledge or understanding of transitional areas or the market processes which both affect and are affected by racial change.

This is not to say that there have been no studies. The literature on residential segregation, on race relations in mixed areas, and on the problems that Negroes face in obtaining satisfactory housing is quite extensive.[2] Many studies have also been made of particular facets of mixed-area markets, particularly price movements, and to a lesser extent, discrimination by lenders.[3] There have been no studies, however, which have examined an interracial market in its entirety, and which have drawn together in one package the numerous demand, supply, and price factors which can intertwine into a variety of patterns of racial change.

Yet the mechanism of transition is the real estate market. Attitudes and beliefs about Negroes expressed here exert considerable control over rates of Negro in-migration, the entry and exodus of white families, and price fluctuations. At the same time, the nature and state of the market itself—the quality of housing, types of structures, tenure, and vacancy rates—have a considerable bearing on the ease with which Negroes enter a white market, and the response which their entry evokes. Thus, whether a particular in-

---

[2] See, for instance, Charles Abrams, *Forbidden Neighbors* (New York: Harper and Brothers, 1955); Henry G. Stetler, *Racial Integration in Private Residential Neighborhoods in Connecticut* (Hartford: State of Connecticut Commission on Civil Rights, 1957); Robert C. Weaver, *The Negro Ghetto* (New York: Harcourt, Brace and Co., 1948).

[3] See particularly, Luigi Laurenti, *Property Values and Race: Studies in Seven Cities* (Berkeley: University of California Press, 1959). See also E. F. Schietinger, "Racial Succession and Changing Property Values in Residential Chicago" (Ph. D. thesis, Department of Sociology, University of Chicago, 1953, dittoed).

terracial housing study be concerned with attitudes, intergroup relations, institutional barriers to Negro entry, or price movements, the real estate market can provide a useful frame of reference. This study, therefore, examines the real estate market in several sections of Philadelphia that have been undergoing transition in recent years in an attempt to reveal more about the conditions that make for racial change and the manner in which market forces shape the transition process.

CHANGES IN PHILADELPHIA'S POPULATION

The racial transition in the areas selected for study is part of a much larger population shift which has been in process for many years in the city as a whole. To understand the change in the racial composition of these study areas, one must be aware of their peculiar or special social, economic, and physical characteristics and of their relationship to the larger scene.

The city of Philadelphia has one of the largest racial minorities, proportionately, of any northern metropolis. In 1950 its 379,000 nonwhites comprised more than 18 percent of the total population.[4] Only New York and Chicago had more Negroes than Philadelphia, and in those cities the proportion of nonwhites to total population was considerably less. Since 1950 the Philadelphia Negro population has grown absolutely to approximately 500,000 and relatively to about 25 percent of the total.[5] Many southern cities cannot match either of these figures.

Unlike many northern urban areas, the presence of a large num-

---

[4] U. S. Census of Population: 1950, vol. II, Characteristics of the Population, part 38, "Pennsylvania." The border cities of Baltimore and Washington had larger proportions of nonwhites than Philadelphia. Newark, with a nonwhite population in excess of 17 percent, was not far behind the Quaker City. According to one estimate, Newark is now more than one-quarter nonwhite, but the figure must remain tentative until the 1960 Census. See Chester Rapkin, Eunice Grier, and George Grier, Group Relations in Newark, 1957, A Report to the Mayor's Commission on Group Relations (New York: Urban Research, September, 1957).

[5] See Leonard Blumberg, "An Estimate of the Nonwhite Population of Philadelphia, 1950-1955," The Urban League of Philadelphia, November, 1956, (mimeo.). Blumberg's estimate of 451,000 for June, 1955, is corroborated by an unpublished estimate of the household population made by the Bureau of the Census in connection with its National Housing Inventory, December, 1956. This sector of the population has expanded by approximately 50,000 since that time.

ber of Negroes is not a recent phenomenon for Philadelphia. As early as 1810, nonwhites constituted over 9 percent of the city's total population.[6] From 1810 to 1870 the number of Negroes moved upward very slowly, but, in the face of heavy waves of European immigration, the ratio of Negro to total population declined to less than 4 percent. This downward trend was reversed during the next twenty years, and since 1890 the increase of nonwhites has taken place at a fairly rapid rate (see Appendix D, tables D-1 and D-2). On a percentage basis, the most significant expansion was from 1910 to 1930, when the Negro population almost tripled. In absolute numbers, however, the largest increases have been felt since 1940. In contrast to the growth of the Negro community, the white sector has remained almost stationary since 1920 and, in fact, appears to be smaller today than it was at that time.[7]

Nonwhites have not only grown in number, they have also risen in economic status. One manifestation has been a steady rise in the rate of homeownership among nonwhites from 4 percent in 1900 to 29 percent in 1950 to an estimated 44 percent in 1956[8] (see Appendix D, table D-3). The purchases by Negroes have been confined almost exclusively to homes in the existing stock. This has been due in part to the failure of builders either to serve the Negro market or to merchandise their construction on a free and equal basis. It has been estimated that of approximately 250,-000 dwelling units constructed in the Philadelphia Standard Metropolitan Area from July, 1946, through June, 1955, less than 3,000 units, or between 1 and 2 percent, were made available to Negroes, despite the fact that well over one-eighth of the metropolitan area population is nonwhite.[9]

The restriction of Negro purchases to the existing supply cannot, however, be blamed on discrimination alone. The vast majority of Negroes, despite their occupational and employment

---

[6] I. Maximilian Martin, *Housing Problems of the Philadelphia Nonwhite Population* (Philadelphia: Isadore Martin, 1953), p. 1.

[7] U. S. Bureau of the Census, *1956 National Housing Inventory*, unpublished data.

[8] *Ibid.*

[9] Slightly more than one-half of the new construction was in Philadelphia. See "New Housing Available to Negroes," Philadelphia Housing Association, April, 1956 (mimeo.).

gains, are still unable to afford new housing. Within the city of Philadelphia itself, where the cheapest new homes command prices in excess of $10,000, only 25,000 of the 126,000 nonwhite families have annual incomes of $5,000 or more.[10] Since many of the Negro householders who do have the resources to purchase new construction are satisfied with their present homes, and since many others would prefer used houses even if they did enter the market, it is obvious that most nonwhite families have not been directly affected by the discriminatory policies of home builders.

The transition of neighborhoods from white to mixed to predominantly Negro occupancy is a process which has been under way in Philadelphia for more than a century and a half. The growth of the Negro population has necessarily resulted in the expansion of their settlements to include previously all-white areas. For years the expansion attracted little notice because it proceeded at an extremely moderate rate and involved areas which whites were happy to abandon. Only when the pressure of population growth and rising incomes caused Negroes to fan out in large numbers into many good residential sections, did their movement receive widespread attention.

The historic center of Negro settlement in Philadelphia was at 6th and Lombard, in the southeast corner of the original town laid out by William Penn.[11] From here and from smaller cores in other inlying sections of the city, Negroes spread into a number of areas, usually replacing the foreign-born families as the latter group moved farther out. A "black belt," such as New York's Harlem, never developed. Instead, the Negro population concentrated in fifteen wards in three separate and distinct sections of the city. In 1950, these areas, all of them older neighborhoods fairly close to the central business district, contained over 80 percent of Philadelphia's Negro population. There were, however, Negroes in all fifty-two wards of the city, and in only five wards were there fewer than one hundred nonwhites (figure 1).

The relatively wide dispersion of Negroes has provided many

---

[10] U. S. Bureau of the Census, *1956 National Housing Inventory,* unpublished data.

[11] W. E. B. Dubois, *The Philadelphia Negro* (Philadelphia: Ginn, 1899).

bases for the expansion of nonwhite neighborhoods in recent years. As a result, transition has not been confined to a few sections, but is occurring in numerous scattered places throughout

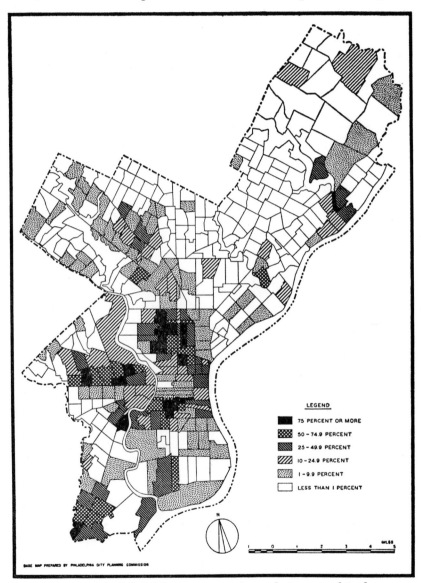

LEGEND

75 PERCENT OR MORE

50 - 74.9 PERCENT

25 - 49.9 PERCENT

10 - 24.9 PERCENT

1 - 9.9 PERCENT

LESS THAN 1 PERCENT

BASE MAP PREPARED BY PHILADELPHIA CITY PLANNING COMMISSION

Fig. 1. City of Philadelphia, percent of population nonwhite by census tracts, 1950.

the city. In 1956, it was estimated that there were no fewer than twenty-six racially changing areas in Philadelphia[12] (figure 2). Of

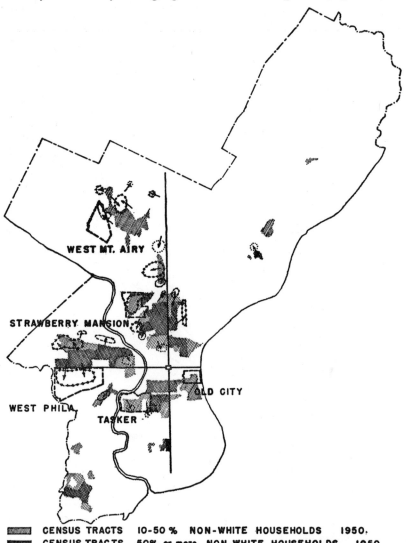

CENSUS TRACTS   10-50 % NON-WHITE HOUSEHOLDS   1950.
CENSUS TRACTS   50% or more NON-WHITE HOUSEHOLDS   1950.
AREAS OF MAJOR CHANGE .1956.   AREAS OF MODERATE CHANGE
AREAS OF MINOR CHANGE .1956   DIRECTION OF CHANGE

Fig. 2. Philadelphia: The study areas, established racially mixed areas, emerging racially mixed areas.

[12] Commission on Human Relations, City of Philadelphia, unpublished material.

this group, four areas containing more than 50,000 dwelling units were chosen for study. These areas—West Philadelphia, Strawberry Mansion, Tasker, and Old City—differed in the rapidity of transition and in the quality of the housing stock. A fifth area, the West Mount Airy section of Germantown, was added later in the study to shed some light on the transition process in upper-income areas (see Appendix A).

The social laboratory provided by the mixed areas enabled us to explore a number of significant questions. Investigations were made of the number of white and Negro families who purchased homes in the areas, the racial composition of the blocks in which the purchases were made, and the demographic composition of the purchasing families. In addition, we learned something about attitudes of white families and their motives for moving to the particular area or dwelling. The financial details of each transaction were also investigated to see if there were any radical departures in the prices paid by and in the mortgage terms available to Negro and white purchasers. The emphasis in the analysis of these data, however, was on the structure of demand and supply so that prices and mortgage terms could be placed in the perspective of the total economic setting. A full account of the methods and techniques utilized is presented in Appendix C.

THE STUDY AREAS

The areas selected for study bear names by which at least a portion of each area is known. Each area represented two attributes as indicated in the tabulation below.

Rate of Racial Transition	Quality of Housing	
	Good	Poor
Fast	West Philadelphia	Strawberry Mansion
Slow	Tasker	Old City

This classification was based upon the quality of housing as given in the 1950 Census and on the proportion of blocks that shifted in racial composition between 1950 and 1955. According to the 1950 Census of Housing, only 2.5 percent of the dwelling units in West Philadelphia and 7.2 percent in Tasker lacked pri-

vate baths or were dilapidated whereas 10.8 percent in Strawberry Mansion and 24.1 in Old City were in the same condition.
The increase in the Negro population between 1950 and 1956 was
almost tenfold in West Philadelphia and even greater in Strawberry Mansion. In contrast, the racial minority in the Old City
remained virtually unchanged, and the growth of the Negro population in Tasker proceeded at a moderate rate. The following
pages present a descriptive sketch of each area and point up some
of the more subtle variations among them.

The West Philadelphia Study Area.—The West Philadelphia
study area, located about two miles due west of downtown
Philadelphia, could almost be described as a city within a
city. It is the residence of over 80,000 persons and within
its two square miles are found 25,000 homes, several large commercial centers, and a number of light industrial establishments.
Over thirty churches and synagogues, thirteen schools, a college,
a few small parks and playgrounds, recreational centers, a library
and a hospital are available to serve the needs of the local population.

A certain amount of physical self-containment is provided by
three of the area's four boundaries. Market Street—broad, largely
commercial, and overhung by an elevated railroad—separates the
area from the predominantly Negro sections to the north. Baltimore Avenue, a heavily traveled commercial artery, forms another natural divider on the south. To the west lies Cobbs Creek
Park. Only at the eastern boundary, 45th Street, could one enter
or leave the area without feeling that a border had been crossed.

West Philadelphia, like the city as a whole, is largely a community of row houses. There are some single-family homes in
semidetached structures, but many of these are so closely spaced
as to be practically indistinguishable from row units. In all, single-
family houses of all types account for two-thirds of the dwelling
units. Most of the structures are quite old. Over 75 percent were
erected between 1900 and 1920. Construction in the area during
the decade of the 1920's was confined principally to 30 to 40 apartment structures, and from 1929 until today only 400 new units
have been added to the stock.

By today's standards, the vast majority of the houses have inadequate fenestration and yard space. Only a few have garages or offstreet parking areas. The intermingling of nonresidential uses and the abrasive effect of heavy through traffic on the major arteries have blighted some sections. Yet despite age and obsolescence, the houses are in good condition and compare favorably with dwellings in other parts of the city. The median value of owner-occupied homes in the area at the time of the 1950 Census was approximately $7,900, whereas the corresponding figure for the entire city was only $6,990.

West Philadelphia has long been regarded as a middle-class section of the city. In 1950 more than half the adults had a high school education and average family income was in the vicinity of $4,000. Over one-quarter of the workers were in professional or managerial occupations. The rate of homeownership was almost 60 percent. By all of these measures—education, income, occupation, and homeownership—West Philadelphia ranked ahead of the city as a whole.

The first residents of the area were of Irish and English descent. They were joined by a large number of German and Russian Jews and by a small group of Greeks and Armenians. The total population reached 81,000 by 1930 and stabilized at approximately that figure for the next twenty years.

The nonwhite population was for many years small and apparently unnoticed. In 1925 it was estimated that only 500 Negroes lived in the area and they were concentrated in the blocks along the northern border contiguous to the Negro and mixed neighborhoods above Market Street.[13] During the 1920's, however, many neighborhoods north of Market and east of 45th Street were experiencing transition, and by the latter half of the decade, the racial transition had reached the study area and was beginning to cause concern among local residents. As early as 1930, when the Negro population was still less than 2 percent of total, successful attempts to thwart Negro entry were reported.[14]

The depression, World War II, and the postwar housing short-

---

[13] See T. J. Woofter, Jr., and Madge Headley Priest, *Negro Housing in Philadelphia* (Philadelphia: Friends' Committee on Interests of the Colored Race, Whittier Center Housing Company, and Philadelphia Housing Association, 1927).

[14] See William Wallace Weaver, "West Philadelphia, a Study of Natural Social Areas" (unpublished Ph.D. thesis, University of Pennsylvania, 1930).

age acted as even more effective deterrents to racial change and, as a result, nonwhite expansion was virtually imperceptible for almost twenty years. In 1950, Negroes, other than resident janitors in the large apartment buildings, were scattered over one-sixth of the blocks, but in only a few blocks were nonwhite households as much as 10 percent of the total.

In the spring of 1950, however, the transition process resumed momentum, first in the vicinity of Chestnut and 58th, and later over a much wider sector. Negro purchases continued at an increasing rate through 1955 at which time nonwhites resided in about three-quarters of all blocks in the area.

Strawberry Mansion.—Strawberry Mansion is an old area located in North Philadelphia, near Fairmont Park. By the late nineteenth century, it was completely developed with houses and small shops. Since that time there has been virtually no new private investment, the new construction consisting entirely of two public housing projects, schools, and community buildings financed by public funds. The area in general conveys an impression of dreariness because of its unimaginative architecture and the overcrowding of land. The harshness of the scene is mitigated by a few streets lined with trees, the only objects that seem to have benefited from the passing of time.

Although the physical environment has in essence altered little over the years, the characteristics of the occupants of the structures have changed considerably. The first settlers were Germans of varying incomes. Those who were in comfortable circumstances resided in the limited number of spacious row houses while the working class families lived in the smaller dwellings more typical of the area. But large or small, these dwellings were solidly built and well maintained in the Germanic tradition of a proper home.

During the early part of this century, the vast migration from Europe set in process the successive occupancy of the housing stock. Jewish people, whose first area of settlement was the Old City and whose economic status had improved, began to enter Strawberry Mansion at the same time that the earlier German residents who had moved to still higher social and economic levels were looking to the prestige areas of Chestnut Hill and the Main Line. By 1930, Russian Jews living in the western half of the study area adjacent to Fairmont Park were the predominant ethnic group. A small Catholic community lived in the northeast, and a variety of nationality groups were to be found in the remainder of the eastern area.

As early as 1900, a Negro community was located a short distance to the southeast of the study area, with some Negro families residing in the interstitial blocks and in the eastern portion of the area itself. Since 1939 the Negro population has moved north and west, and today Negro families live in almost every block of the study area. Although the white population has been decreasing, many white families, particularly in the northwestern portion, have remained. This portion of the study area, the last to experience Negro occupancy, has many elderly residents who are attached to their synagogues and special Jewish shops or who are too poor to move away. Along the northern boundary further to the east there is a small Italian community which maintains strong bonds to parish and neighborhood. There are, in addition, many white families in the area who do not appear tied to any obvious characteristic of the neighborhood.

The gradual decline in the level of living in the area is seen in the history of the large row houses. Acquired from their original German occupants, many of these structures were converted into doctors' rows. With the spread of Negro occupancy, these houses were purchased by slum landlords and subdivided into tiny dwelling units which, for the most part, contain neither private bath nor kitchen and are often over-occupied. But despite the substandard quality of these dwellings, the rental per square foot of space is quite high.

Of the four study areas, Strawberry Mansion is evidently in the latest stage of transition physically and racially. Filled as it is with older houses and containing a minimum of open space, the prognosis cannot be too favorable. It would appear that the occupants of this area will be limited to families whose choice is narrowed by inadequate income or whose market is circumscribed by virtue of the color of their skin.

Tasker.—Fifty years ago the Tasker area must indeed have been a dreary place in which to live. The eastern section consisted of row houses constructed for working class families during the latter half of the nineteenth century, and the western portion was a depressing backwork of mosquito swamps, gas works, and garbage dumps. Since that time the government filled the land and later constructed more than 1,000 public housing units, religious structures and parochial schools were built by the Catholic Church, and there has been a considerable amount of private investment in row house developments, particularly since the end of the Second World War. Today, the area is predominantly residential containing homes of low cost but relatively good quality. The atmosphere, however, is blighted by the smells, sounds, and sights of an industrial concentration located nearby.

The composition of the white population has changed very little over the years. The occupants are of Irish and Italian stock for the most part, with a sprinkling of Poles and Russians. The area has had a firm hold on its population as a result of the close family ties and the strong influence of tradition particularly observable among the Italian residents of the community. The area also has many attractive church-associated facilities and activities, and is within easy access to industrial employment.

Records of thirty years ago show many predominantly Negro blocks located along the railroad on the northern boundary and the elevated structure close to the eastern boundary of the Tasker area. Pressure from Negroes to the north, who sought the relatively low-cost housing of the study area, was somewhat relieved by opening up blocks adjacent to the established Negro strips. These blocks became virtually all Negro in a short time, but because they were few in number, the proportion of Negroes residing in the area during the 1925–1945 period showed just a slight upward drift. Since the end of World War II, the public housing project which was formerly all white has become occupied by both Negro and white families, and local building and loan associations have financed homes for Negroes on many blocks previously "out of bounds." Whether the ability and desire of the Negroes to purchase homes in this area and the interest of the whites in maintaining the character of the neighborhood will produce a scattered racial pattern or an extension of the Negro ghetto in all or part of the area is problematical at this time.

Old City.—The Old City, as its name implies, is one of the earliest areas of settlement in Philadelphia. In the northern portion of the area are to be found Independence Hall and other significant historical buildings of the same era. Here, too, are a sprinkling of fine homes of Philadelphia's first families some of which are still occupied by their descendants. For over a century, this portion of the study area was one of the most fashionable sections of the city, but behind the handsome buildings the narrow back alleys were crowded with servants and prior to that, slaves. During colonial times and in the early days of the republic, the streets to the south were lined with the homes of growing numbers of freedmen who formed a concentration which became the first center of Negro population in Philadelphia.

Unlike the other three study areas, the major portion of land in Old City today is devoted to nonresidential uses. On the north are many office buildings of the financial and insurance district which grew up on the streets adjoining State House Row. To the east are docks and warehouses, while South Street, the lower boundary, forms the axis of one of the declining shopping areas in Philadelphia.

To the eye the Old City presents many contrasts, as one would expect from its history and location. Walking down the tree-lined streets, turning into the narrow alleys, and coming upon the busy docks and market streets, one is impressed by the suddenness with which the scene shifts at each turning, an experience that is tempered by the unity of homogeneous strips of row houses. However, these, too, vary from blocks of luxurious town houses of twelve to fifteen rooms to the two- or three-room bandbox whose dimensions and plan were inadequate even at the time of construction. In short, the Old City area is polyglot in population, mixed in architecture, and marked by the interplay of a variety of cultural strains.

II

The Number and Spatial Distribution
of Purchasers

The inception of this study was accompanied by more than the usual quota of misgivings. Many observers thought that there would be difficulty in locating any white purchasers in the study areas and that if some were found the number would be so small as to be of little consequence. Our field studies, however, revealed white purchasers in large numbers, and this in itself is one of the most significant findings of the entire investigation.

This chapter presents the findings on the number of purchasers and location of purchases in each area in 1955. Particular attention is paid to the distribution of acquisitions by race, and the extent to which the racial composition of the area and its rate of change tends to shape these distributions.

In order to acquire the necessary data, a list was compiled of all property transfers in the study areas that were recorded during the year 1955 and a transcription made of the details of each transaction. Later the racial characteristics of the purchasers were identified. Through field inspection the racial composition of every block and street front in the area was determined and mapped. This was a long and arduous process, the details of which are presented step by step in Appendix C.

NUMBER OF PURCHASES

In 1955 there were 2,340 bona fide transfers of ownership of residential property in the four mixed areas, of which 2,017 involved acquisition for owner-occupancy.[1] The group of home purchasers consisted of 443 white and 1,574 Negro families. Although three and one-half times as many Negroes as whites purchased houses in the areas, the number of whites who did so is impressive. This sheds doubt on the premise that once Negroes enter a neighborhood, no white will purchase in the area thereafter.

TABLE 1

RACE OF PURCHASER IN FOUR MIXED AREAS, 1955

Area	Owner occupant				Absentee owner		Total	
	White		Negro					
	No.	Pct.	No.	Pct.	No.	Pct.	No.	Pct.
West Philadelphia	286	22	864	68	132	10	1,282	100
Tasker	128	50	70	27	58	23	256	100
Strawberry Mansion	25	3	640	81	131	16	796	100
Old City	4	*	...	...	2	*	6	*
All Areas	443	19	1,574	67	323	14	2,340	100

*Percentages not meaningful, numbers too small.

There was a marked difference in the proportion of purchases by race among the study areas (table 1). In West Philadelphia, an area undergoing rapid change and where housing is of good quality, the ratio of Negro to white purchasers for owner-occupancy was three to one, roughly the same as for all areas. In Tasker, where housing is good but the change is slow, the white buyers outnumbered the Negroes by two to one. In the Strawberry Mansion area, where the quality of dwellings is rapidly declining, twenty-seven times as many Negroes as whites were purchasers. In the Old City, where change is slow and housing poor, there appears to have been no market at all for residential properties during 1955. Only six properties of this type were sold in that year, and two of these were acquired for investment rather than for occupancy.

A white family's decision to purchase a house in a mixed area should not be confused with the decision of a resident family to remain in the area after it has become mixed. In the first case, the family is presumed to be aware of the complexion of the area

[1] Transfers to clear title, or between members of the same household, or to heirs were eliminated, as were bona fide sales of nonresidential properties and multi-family structures.

before the purchase is made, and there is the real alternative of choosing a house in another area which may be all white. If the family is seeking a low or moderately priced house, its choice is limited. But even considering this limitation and accepting the assumption that it is more likely for home-owning Negro families to be found in such areas, there are nevertheless many places within this price range in which the population is entirely white. Thus, for one or another reason, the white family that purchases in a mixed area sees fit to do so despite the fact that alternatives are available. Moreover, virtually all of the purchasing families have the option of remaining where they are.

In making the decision to purchase a house in a mixed area, a family also incurs the type of commitments that accompany home purchase anywhere. The acquisition of a dwelling involves the largest single investment that a family is likely to experience and the assumption of a fixed long-term mortgage obligation. And, what may be more important in mixed areas, a family commits itself to living in the house for a protracted period of time.

As we shall see in a later section of this report, the previous place of residence of some of the white purchasers was in a mixed area. It has been suggested that they therefore had the dubious choice of remaining in such an area or moving to another with similar population characteristics. But these families, too, had the opportunity to choose dwellings in an all-white neighborhood, of which there are many in Philadelphia. Very few purchasers were under an irresistible compulsion to move, let alone buy a house. Only a handful were new arrivals in Philadelphia, and no one had been dispossessed from his former home.

The family that has resided in an area prior to its racial transition and considers leaving when it becomes mixed is confronted with a decision of a different order. If the family had been planning to move prior to the change in the neighborhood but had not as yet made any steps in that direction, racial transition might galvanize the family into action. But if such plans had not been present, then we may assume that the family was reasonably satisfied with its home and neighborhood. The family may have a sentimental attachment to the home by virtue of its association with the family's history. Friendships may have developed with neighbors and with the neighbors' children. Other ties of varying degrees of profundity may have matured over the years between the family and the church, the youngster and the school, or the housewife and the shops in which she trades—all of which tend to bind the family to the area.

Moving from such a situation means the establishment of a whole new set of relationships, the expenditure of time and effort necessary to find a new home, the disorganization of packing and moving, and the incurrence of considerable expense. In addition to the cost of transporting the household effects, expenditures for furniture and other items are necessary to put the new home in order.

Thus, the decision to remain in an area after it becomes mixed is heavily influenced by the forces of attraction, buttressed by the fact that it is always easier to remain passive than to act. It takes either an inordinate response to the entrance of Negroes or a disappearance of the forces of attraction to impel a white family to move under these circumstances. The community ties are, of course, considerably weakened if the old population leaves the area, because friends and institutions go with them. In particular, the generation of panic in a neighborhood, be it spontaneous or induced, not only increases the potential volume of real estate sales, but it also threatens to strip the area of its old population and to disrupt both the formal and informal neighborhood institutions. This threat weakens the attractive power of the area and tends to cause many who would otherwise be inclined to remain to join the exodus.

In short then, the decision to purchase into a mixed area is a positive act taken in the face of alternatives and involving significant commitments. The decision to remain in a mixed area is a passive response the strength of which is contingent upon the ties to the area, the likelihood of their persistence, and the economic circumstances of the family.

LOCATION OF PURCHASES

If the Negro and white population were homogeneously distributed in each of the study areas, then the statistics on the incidence of purchase presented in the preceding section would need no further analysis. Each section, block, and street front would contain the average mixture of white and Negro families and each purchasing family would have acquired a dwelling in a location that promised the same racial environment. The distribution of population in these areas, however, is not uniform. There are sections that are occupied almost exclusively by one or another of the racial groups, and within the mixed sections a wide range exists in the proportion of Negro or white persons to total population. Presumably, therefore, white purchasers could choose among a variety of racial environments, even within a mixed area. The breadth of the choice is, of course, limited by the number and spatial distribution of white, Negro, and mixed blocks.

In order to determine where the purchases were made and to derive some intimations of the influence of the proximity of Negro families on white demand, the data were examined from several different points of view. First we looked at the subareas in which purchases were made, then at the block and those immediately surrounding the place of purchase, and last, at the street front.

The analysis that was undertaken was limited, both in precision and in scope, by the absence of detailed population data for 1955, the year of the study. Because of changes that had occurred in the areas, 1950 census data were obsolete, at least for the areas undergoing rapid change, and the budget for the study precluded a replication of the census, even for the limited number of demographic and housing characteristics that were of interest to us. By drawing upon various sources of information and by supplementary field inspection, however, it was possible to identify the racial characteristics of the residents of each block in the area (see Appendix C). In addition, for each white purchase the racial characteristics of street fronts on which the purchase was made and the front directly across the street were noted. Blocks and street fronts were then classified into three groups: those that were all white, those that were all Negro, and those that were mixed. No further subdivision of the mixed designation was possible. One Negro family on a block or street front otherwise all white, or vice versa, was sufficient to place it in the mixed category. By and large, however, there was more than token representation of families in the smaller racial group.

RACIAL ZONES

From maps prepared to show the racial category into which blocks were classified, it became evident that there was a tendency for white and mixed blocks to cluster in contiguous groups or bands. These groups were delineated for further study by subdividing each area into two broad subareas, a white zone and a mixed zone. The relative ethnic density of blocks or street fronts in the mixed zone tends to be correlated with the location of the block within the zone and with the time lapse since the entry of Negroes occurred. The blocks entirely occupied by Negro families were few in number and were located in the mixed zone. In each of the two zones, some blocks which fell into the other category were to be found. The incidence of all-white blocks in the mixed zones was relatively rare, while mixed blocks were to be found in the white zones with somewhat greater frequency.

These zones were of analytical significance for only two of the four study areas—West Philadelphia and Tasker. In Strawberry Mansion virtually all of the blocks fell into the mixed zone. In Old City the dearth of transactions made detailed study meaningless.

The mixed zone in West Philadelphia included approximately 70 percent of the blocks that contained dwelling units (figure 3). Eighty-three percent of the transfers occurred in this zone, and of these 81 percent were to Negro home purchasers. Thirty-five percent of all purchases by white families in the entire area were in this zone as were almost four-fifths of the acquisitions for purposes other than owner-occupancy (table 2).

In the Tasker area, where approximately 60 percent of the blocks fell in the mixed zones, transfers were divided equally between the mixed and the white zone (figure 4). Sales in the mixed zone were distributed as follows: 15 percent to white families, 57 percent to Negro families, and 28 percent to absentees. This zone accounted for 15 percent of all of the white purchasers in the Tasker area and 62 percent of the properties acquired by absentee owners for investment or speculative purposes (table 3).

From the foregoing presentation it is evident that a more than

TABLE 2

NUMBER AND PERCENT OF PURCHASERS BY TYPE AND RACE AND BY RACIAL ZONE, WEST PHILADELPHIA, 1955

Type and race of purchaser	White zone			Mixed zone			Total area		
	Number	Percent of purchasers in zone	Percent of purchasers in total	Number	Percent of purchasers in zone	Percent of purchasers in total	Number	Percent of purchasers in all zones	Percent of purchasers in total area
Owner-occupant									
White	187	86.1	65.4	99	9.3	34.6	286	22.3	100.0
Negro	1	.5	.1	863	81.0	99.9	864	67.4	100.0
Absentee	29	13.4	22.0	103	9.7	78.0	132	10.3	100.0
Total	217	100.0	16.9	1,065	100.0	83.1	1,282	100.0	100.0

TABLE 3

NUMBER AND PERCENT OF PURCHASERS BY TYPE AND RACE AND BY RACIAL ZONE, TASKER, 1955

Type and race of purchaser	White zone			Mixed zone			Total area		
	Number	Percent of purchasers in zone	Percent of purchasers in total area	Number	Percent of purchasers in zone	Percent of purchasers in total area	Number	Percent of purchasers in all zones	Percent of purchasers in total area
Owner-occupant									
White	110	82.7	85.9	18	14.6	14.1	128	50.0	100.0
Negro	0	0	0	70	56.9	100.0	70	27.3	100.0
Absentee	23	17.3	37.9	35	28.5	62.1	58	22.7	100.0
Total	133	100.0	51.6	123	100.0	48.4	256	100.0	100.0

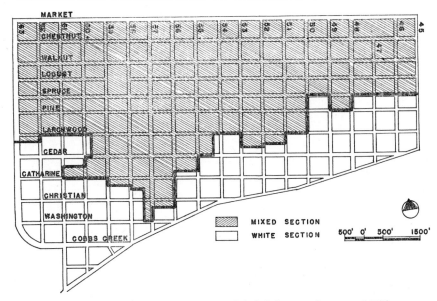

Fig. 3. Racial sections, West Philadelphia study area, 1955.

proportionate number of white purchasers tended to purchase in the white zones. In West Philadelphia, 65 percent of all the white purchases took place in the white zone, which included only 30 percent of the blocks. In Tasker, the white zone included 40 percent of the blocks and accounted for 86 percent of the purchases made by white families in the entire area. In Strawberry Mansion, on the other hand, where all but four widely separated blocks were mixed, all of the white purchases were made in the mixed blocks.

MIXED BLOCKS

The second stage in the analysis of the locational distribution of purchasers consisted of going from large generalized zones to an examination of the blocks in which purchases were made. Here there was an attempt to determine the extent to which white purchases occurred on blocks that were mixed as against those that occurred on blocks that were occupied entirely by white persons at the time of acquisition.

The unit of measurement that was selected for this phase of

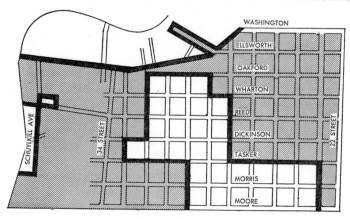

TASKER AREA

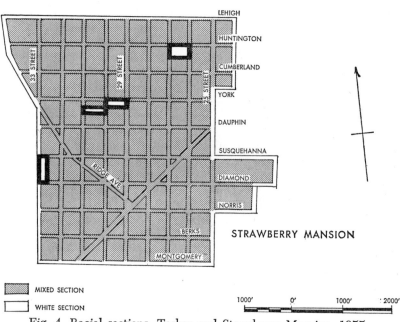

STRAWBERRY MANSION

▨ MIXED SECTION

☐ WHITE SECTION

1000' 0' 1000' : 2000'

Fig. 4. Racial sections, Tasker and Strawberry Mansion, 1955.

the analysis consisted of five contiguous blocks in the shape of a cross in which the house acquired by the white purchaser was located in the central block. If any one of the five blocks were mixed in occupancy, then the entire group was classified as mixed. This mode of classification yielded results that differed from the previous zonal analysis by virtue of the fact that some mixed blocks were to be found in the white zone and vice versa. Moreover, several white purchasers in the border blocks of the white zone purchased dwellings across the street from a mixed block.

A total of 320 white families purchased homes on the same block or on a block adjacent to one in which Negro families resided (table 4). This number constituted 72 percent of the total

TABLE 4

PURCHASES BY WHITES FOR OWNER-OCCUPANCY IN MIXED BLOCKS OR BLOCKS ADJACENT TO MIXED BLOCKS, 1955

Study area	Number	Percent of total white purchasers
West Philadelphia	198	69
Tasker	93	73
Strawberry Mansion	25	100
Old City	4	100
Total	320	72

white purchasers in all of the study areas. In each study area, the number of purchasers living on the same or adjacent block with Negroes formed more than two-thirds of the total white purchaser group.

We thus see that the large majority of white purchases were made in locations that were no more than three linear blocks away from a Negro residence. Had a nine-block unit of measurement been selected (a three by three square with the purchase in the central block), the proportion would have been considerably higher. As it is, a detailed examination of the actual location of each of the purchases revealed that a substantial proportion of them were made within one or two blocks from a resident Negro family.

MIXED STREET FRONTS

In order to examine the effect of proximity in greater detail, we counted the number of white families who purchased homes on the same street front or directly across the street from Negro residents. Although it is unlikely, it is quite possible for a white family residing on or next to a mixed block to encounter a Negro resident only rarely in the routine course of events. On a mixed street front at very least the Negro family is visible and the crossing of paths is virtually inevitable.

Units facing each other across the street were chosen in preference to those that sit perpendicular to each other, or back to back in a block. Merton and others have shown that under ordinary circumstances the occupants of facing dwellings are more likely to become acquainted than families whose houses have some other orientation. In large measure this is due to the fact that the occupants will likely chance upon each other often in the course of performing household tasks and in each day's coming and going.[2]

In the study areas, purchase of a residence on a mixed street front has an added significance. A large proportion of the single-family housing stock consists of row houses which are highly homogeneous on any given street. Since means of distinguishing one unit from another on the block are very limited, the acquisition of a row house constitutes public pronouncement of lack of exclusiveness and the absence of separation from one's neighbors. This does not necessarily imply any rapport or identification with other families on the block, but it is qualitatively different from the situation in which a white family will purchase the mansion on the hill or move into a luxurious apartment house that is adjacent to less pretentious structures occupied by Negroes. In these situations the disparity between the quality and price of the houses occupied by Negroes and whites symbolizes wide differences in social and economic status. In the case of the row house, this physical means of distinguishing between the status of the two groups does not exist. In fact, if there is any symbolism at all in the row of attached structures, it is association, the absence of differences, and the identity of status.[3]

In all four study areas slightly more than one-fourth of the white purchasers acquired dwellings on the same street front or

---

[2] Robert K. Merton, "The Social Psychology of Housing," in W. Dennis, *Current Trends in Social Psychology* (Pittsburgh: University of Pittsburgh Press, 1948); L. Festinger, S. Shachter, and K. Back, *Social Pressures in Informal Groups* (New York: Harper and Brothers, 1950).

[3] It must be remembered, however, that the row house in Philadelphia is a commonplace, constituting three-fourths of all dwelling units in 1950. Since this type of unit is so widespread, it may be that Philadelphians are less sensitive to its outward appearance of uniformity.

facing a street front on which Negro families lived, while the remainder purchased on all-white street fronts and facing street fronts.[4] Virtually all of the Negro purchases (98 percent) were on streets with at least one white family in residence. Almost three-quarters of the purchases by absentee owners were on mixed streets, one-fifth were on white streets, and 8 percent on streets entirely occupied by Negroes (table 5).

TABLE 5

NUMBER AND PERCENT OF TRANSFERS BY RACE AND TYPE OF PURCHASER
AND RACIAL CHARACTERISTIC OF STREET, ALL STUDY AREAS, 1955

Race and type of purchaser	Racial characteristic of street						Total transfers	
	White		Mixed		Negro			
	No.	Pct.	No.	Pct.	No.	Pct.	No.	Pct.
Owner-occupant								
White	324	73.1	119	26.9	...	...	443	100.0
Negro	...	...	1,540	97.8	34	2.2	1,574	100.0
Absentee	64	19.8	232	71.8	27	8.4	323	100.0
Total	388	16.6	1,891	80.8	61	2.6	2,340	100.0

It is by now evident that the proximity effect is unquestionably present. Out of a total of 443 residences acquired by white families in the four mixed areas in 1955, 320, or 72 percent, were located on or adjacent to mixed blocks within these areas, and 119, or 27 percent, were on or directly opposite a mixed street. Thus, it appears that the greater the proximity of Negroes, the smaller will be the proportion of white purchasers within any mixed area. The striking fact to emerge from this sea of statistics is not the sharp drop-off in the proportion of white purchasers, an observation that was anticipated, but the fact that 119 white families chose to purchase and reside on a mixed street, an observation that was not anticipated.

BLOCKS WITH NEGRO AND WHITE PURCHASES

Another measure of the influence of racial change on demand was the extent to which Negro and white purchases were made on the same block during 1955. In West Philadelphia, the only study area for which this type of analysis was performed, it was found

---

[4] The terms street and street front will both be used henceforth to refer to the street front and facing street front.

that three-fourths of the white purchases occurred in blocks in which no Negro purchases were made in that year, and a similar proportion of Negro families purchased in blocks in which there were no white purchasers in 1955 (table 6). One quarter of the

TABLE 6

RACIAL DISTRIBUTION OF PURCHASERS, BY BLOCK, WEST PHILADELPHIA, 1955

Race of Purchasers	Purchases						Blocks	
	Total		White		Negro			
	No.	Pct.	No.	Pct.	No.	Pct.	No.	Pct.
White only	216	18	216	76	...	...	116	32
Negro only	662	58	...	...	662	77	148	40
White and Negro	272	24	70	24	202	23	48	12
No purchasers	...	...	...	...	...	...	60	16
Total	1,150	100	286	100	864	100	372	100

purchases made by each of the groups, therefore, took place on blocks in which there was at least one acquisition by a family of the other racial group in the course of the year. In absolute numbers, purchases on blocks that had both white and Negro buyers in 1955 were made by 70 white families and 202 Negro families, or a ratio of one to three. Examining the incidence of purchase by block, we find that out of a total of 312 blocks, there were 116 blocks in which there were white but no Negro purchasers, 148 in which there were Negro but no white purchaser, 48 in which both Negroes and whites acquired houses, and 60 in which no purchases for owner-occupancy occurred.

An examination of table 7 reveals some further information about blocks in which both Negroes and whites purchased homes in 1955. First, as the number of Negroes purchasing in a block in-

TABLE 7

DISTRIBUTION OF BLOCKS BY NUMBER OF WHITE AND NEGRO
PURCHASERS IN EACH BLOCK, WEST PHILADELPHIA, 1955

Number of white purchasers	Number of Negro purchasers					
	0	1	2	3	4	5 or more
0	60	27	28	19	22	52
1	59	4	5	7	3	12
2	30	9	1	0	0	2
3	14	3	0	1	1	0
4	11	0	0	0	0	0
5 or more	2	0	0	0	0	0

creased, the incidence of white purchasers declined; second, some white purchasers were to be found on blocks in which five or more Negro families acquired homes in the course of the year. Since the discussion in this section has been limited to the experience in West Philadelphia, it may be well to summarize the observations for this area. Out of a total of 286 houses acquired by white purchasers in 1955, 198 were located on or adjacent to mixed blocks, and 75 of these were on the same street front or directly across the street from Negro residents. One hundred white families acquired homes on blocks that had become mixed between 1950 and 1955, and 70 of these families purchased houses on blocks into which Negroes were moving as homeowners in that year.

THE PROBLEM OF ADJACENCY

From the point of view of attaining some degree of stability in the racial composition of an area, perhaps the most strategic question of all is related to the willingness of white families to acquire homes directly adjacent to those occupied by Negroes. Transfers in West Philadelphia were investigated to determine the race and the precise date of occupancy of each of the families who resided in a home adjacent to that acquired by a white purchaser. The white purchasers who resided next door to Negroes and whose occupancy followed that of the Negro family were then identified. It was thus possible to eliminate those situations in which Negro families may have taken title to the dwelling prior to the acquisition of the adjacent home by the white, but where the Negro's race was unknown until he took occupancy of the dwelling.

In all, out of 286 homes purchased by white families in West Philadelphia in 1955, only two were definitely acquired next door to an already resident Negro family. In two additional cases, there was some question about the priority of occupancy. In each of the two uncertain cases the Negro family occupied the adjacent single-family unit as a renter and would presumably have shorter tenure than that of an owner.

Although the number of such purchases is unquestionably extremely low, no firm way of indicating its true statistical meaning is available. The development of such a measure would require a knowledge of the number of homes available for sale that were located next to Negro residences, and there was no reliable way of obtaining this figure. The numerator but not the denominator was available to express the expected incidence of such purchases in probability terms. Casual impressions, however, lead to the conclusion that two to four purchases are far below the theoretically expected number.

The fact that whites show a reluctance to purchase a dwelling next to one occupied by a Negro has profound implications for the future racial composition of an area. For a mixed area to achieve some degree of stability in the racial composition of its population, it is necessary for the number of white (or Negro) families who come into the area to balance the number of white (or Negro) families who leave. If this does not occur, and the proportion of in-migrants in one racial group is greater than the proportion of that group among the out-migrants, the area must in due course become largely occupied by one or the other of the racial groups.

It would be an elaboration of the obvious to develop a probability model to demonstrate the results of a situation in which virtually no whites are willing to purchase a dwelling next door to a Negro family, but where Negroes are ready to acquire a house regardless of the race of the next door neighbor. Sooner or later, each of the houses occupied by whites will come on the market and virtually all of those adjacent to a residence occupied by Negroes will find only Negro purchasers. Unless this pattern is interrupted, in time each home on the block will be located next to one occupied by Negroes and, eventually, most of the area will find itself inhabited by nonwhites.

There is an intimation of a change in this pattern or at least in its effect. If it were true, as widely held, that no white would buy into an area once the transition process had begun, considering the problem of adjacency would be a futile academic exercise. Since it has been found, however, that an appreciable number of whites did buy into mixed areas and on mixed blocks, the entire question is cast in a different light. Most of the whites who purchased into the area knew (as will be seen in a later chapter) that Negroes were in residence and that some order of transition was in process. Although these families did not purchase next door to a Negro, they knowingly exposed themselves to the real possibility that, in time, such a contingency would materialize. Whether they planned to remain or even considered what they would do under such circumstances is, of course, impossible to say. It is known, however, that home-purchasing families are not particularly mobile and that they rarely acquire a home with the intention of moving from it within a short period of time.

III

Characteristics, Motivations, and Attitudes of White Buyers

In order to gain additional understanding of the structure of demand for dwellings in racially mixed areas, the characteristics of white purchasers were investigated. It has frequently been alleged that although a few white families will, indeed, buy homes in transitional neighborhoods, these families constitute a peculiar and quite unrepresentative sector of total demand. The primary objective of this section of the study therefore was to ascertain whether the white purchasers in these areas were a special group in the population by virtue of their demographic characteristics, their motivations for purchase, or their attitudes about mixed areas.

To answer these questions, interviews were conducted with 194 white families who, in 1955, purchased and occupied single-family dwelling units on a racially mixed block or one block removed from a mixed block. An additional group of 100 white families who, in 1955, rented dwellings on mixed blocks in the West Philadelphia area were also located and interviewed. To secure comparable information on the nonwhite in-migrants, interviews were held with 196 Negro families who purchased and occupied single-family dwelling units within the study area in 1955.[1]

---

[1] It is suggested that differences in universe and sample size be kept in mind throughout the report, since proportions are often employed in place of number of cases.

HOUSEHOLD CHARACTERISTICS

The home-purchasing families appeared in most respects to be characteristic of the white resident and home-buying population at large and resembled in many ways the white residents in the areas into which they purchased. Families who rented apartments were typical of the existing rental group in the area. The renters on the average were somewhat older, had more formal education, and were of higher income than the white home purchasers. On the average, there was great similarity between Negro and white home purchasers, but Negro families tended to show a greater range of variation within each attribute than whites.

Families with preschool or school age children are usually considered the least likely candidates for housing in a mixed area. Arnold Rose,[2] among others, has shown that parents of young children are unhappy about living in mixed areas and that their anxieties increase as the children progress to the junior high school level. Our findings show that, at least in some cases, either there is no concern or else this anxiety does not affect home purchase if the dwelling and location meet other requirements. Almost three-quarters of all the white purchasers had children under 18 years old and half had children of school age (table 8).[3] By comparison approximately 60 percent of all home purchasers in Philadelphia in 1955 and 1956 had children under 18 and only 36 percent had youngsters of school age. The comparable proportions for white households in Philadelphia were 57 percent and 26 percent respectively.[4] Among the white purchasers, median household size was 3.9, while for the city of Philadelphia during 1956 the median for owner-occupied households was 3.8 and for recent home purchasers 4.2.[5]

As might be expected from our knowledge of the type of household that can be found in the home-buying market, the family

---

[2] Arnold M. Rose, Frank J. Atelsek, and Lawrence R. McDonald, "Neighborhood Reactions to Isolated Negro Residents: An Alternative to Invasion and Succession," *American Sociological Review*, vol. 18, no. 5 (October, 1953), 497-507.

[3] For detailed data on each characteristic see appendix tables.

[4] U. S. Bureau of the Census, *1956 National Housing Inventory*, Philadelphia Supplement, unpublished data.

[5] *Ibid.*

TABLE 8

CHARACTERISTICS OF HOME-PURCHASING FAMILIES IN MIXED AREAS COMPARED WITH
ALL HOUSEHOLDS AND RECENT HOME PURCHASERS IN PHILADELPHIA, 1955–1956

Characteristic	Mixed area purchasers		Recent home purchasers (Philadelphia total)	All households	
	White	Negro		White	Total
Median age of household head (years)	36	34	42	51	49
Median family income (dollars)	4,830	4,850	5,320	4,850	4,520
	PERCENT				
Households with children	73	60	59	41	57
Households with school age children	50	44	36	27	26
Husband/Wife households	88	86	85	71	68
Occupation of household head Professional and managerial	15	9	10	24	20
Clerical and sales	15	13	35	19	17
Craftsmen and foremen	28	19	6	25	23
Service workers, laborers and others	42	54	49	32	40
Religious preference of household head					
Catholic	68	NA	51	57	44
Protestant	20	NA	16	27	43
Jewish	11	NA	29	14	11
Other and NA	1	NA	3	2	2

with both husband and wife present constituted the overwhelming majority of households. Negro purchasers on the whole revealed the same pattern of household composition, except for a slightly larger proportion of unrelated persons. White renters differed from the purchasers in that almost one-quarter consisted of unrelated individuals rather than husband and wife families.

One could infer from the large number of families with children that a substantial proportion of young families would be found among the purchasers. In fact, two out of three heads of households were under 45 years of age, a proportion approximately the same as that of the home-buying population at large.[6]

Almost one-half of the respondents in each area had completed

[6] *Ibid.*

primary and some portion of secondary school, and the level of educational attainment was quite similar to that of the resident population of the areas in 1950.

The occupational distribution of the heads of the white households showed no unusual concentration in professional or other groups that might be associated with special views on racial matters. Professional, proprietor, and managerial positions were held by 16 percent of the purchasers. In all four areas, some purchasers were in each occupational category, with slightly less than half the household heads employed as craftsmen, foremen, or operatives. The white renters were more heavily represented in the higher-status occupations and in the retired groups. The occupations of Negro purchasers included fewer professional or retired persons and more operatives and laborers.

Households with more than one full-time worker were also identified in the interviews. Almost one-third of the white purchasers replied "yes" to the question, "Does anyone else in the household work full time?" The white renters interviewed conformed quite closely to the white purchasers. On the other hand, almost half the Negro purchasers' households contained secondary workers. This larger proportion is in part explained by differences in family composition and age and by the lower incomes of Negro household heads.

Within the white households, many of the secondary workers were children or other relatives of the head, and the proportion of housewives who were not gainfully employed was therefore larger than the proportion of households with secondary workers would appear to indicate. The housewife spends most of her time in and around the house and comes in frequent contact with her neighbors in the course of undertaking her daily chores. On her, perhaps more than on her employed spouse, rests the burden of maintaining neighborly relationships with other residents of the areas in a variety of social situations. Although she may select the individuals with whom she wishes to maintain acquaintanceship or cultivate a friendship, her path must perforce cross that of others not of her choice, a condition that may lead to trivial but inescapable social exchange.

Because of the large proportion of respondents who refused to divulge information on their income, it is impossible to present more than casual impressions on this subject. By and large, it appeared that the income of the white home purchasers was somewhat above the average for the area in which they purchased and for the city as a whole. In part, the income level is a function of the incidence of secondary wage earners in the households.

The white purchasers in mixed areas included much the same proportion of foreign-born persons resident in the city as a whole. In 1950, about one in seven of Philadelphia's white population was born abroad whereas among the 1955 white purchasers one in six persons fell into this category. The interviews revealed that in fully one-half of the cases the parents of the white householders were born abroad. This observation, coupled with the data on religion presented below, suggests that particular ethnic groups were attracted to each of the study areas.

The religious preferences of the white home purchasers in mixed areas were only slightly different from those of the population at large. Sixty-eight percent of the white household heads were Roman Catholic, 20 percent Protestant, and 11 percent Jewish. The purchasers thus included a higher proportion of Catholics than was found in the city at large, where the corresponding ratios for the white population were 57 percent Catholic, 27 percent Protestant, and 14 percent Jewish. The religious distribution of the purchasing families, however, was more or less in keeping with the composition of the areas. This was evident in Tasker and in West Philadelphia, where the Catholic population appears to have gravitated to the nodes which existed previously.

The incidence of overt hostility toward Negroes in Polish, Italian, and Irish areas of several cities[7] has led many to assume that the Catholic group is the least likely to purchase dwellings in mixed areas. This phenomenon, described in several scholarly works,[8] is by no means universal and such attitudes and behavior patterns, where they exist, may not prevent purchases in mixed

---

[7] Charles Abrams, *Forbidden Neighbors* (New York: Harper and Brothers, 1955), pp. 103-119, and Hannah Lees, "How Philadelphia Stopped a Race Riot," *The Reporter*, vol. 12, no. 11 (June 2, 1955), p. 26.

[8] B. M. Kramer, "Residential Contact as a Determinant of Attitudes toward Negroes" (unpublished Ph.D. thesis, Harvard University, 1951), for example.

areas by Catholic families, provided there are a sufficient number of the usual factors of attraction in the house or neighborhood.

The national and religious backgrounds of the white purchasers may be associated with special motives for coming to the area, a subject that is discussed in the next section. The religious distribution of the purchasers may also explain why many families with school age children purchased into the mixed areas. Since the majority of these families were Catholic, they were likely to send their children to one of the numerous parochial schools which at that time were attended by only a handful of Negroes.

In summary, the section of the population that purchased homes in racially mixed areas was roughly comparable to the population at large and quite similar to the resident population of the areas into which they moved. The decline in the number of white purchasers associated with Negro entry into residential areas evidently was not accounted for by any special or peculiar group in the population, just as the demand that remained apparently cannot be explained too well by reference to demographic variables.

The Negro purchaser group bore a close similarity to the white purchasers and compared favorably in income and family composition with the resident Negro population. White renters were in strong contrast to both the Negro and white home purchasers. The renter households contained fewer children, a greater proportion of household heads under thirty and above fifty years of age, a higher proportion of unrelated-person households, a slightly higher proportion of persons with some years of college, but a substantially lower total family income. Most of these differences are to be found between owners and renters generally.

REASONS FOR PURCHASE

The survey was also designed to discover whether white purchasers in the racially mixed areas had a unique motive for living in these neighborhoods, or a motive that was so impelling that it compensated for any resistance the home buyers might have had to the mixed character of the area. For example, a shopkeeper who opens early and closes late may find it essential to live adjacent to his place of business. A man may feel compelled to move near his aged and ill mother, or a divinity student who works part-time may choose to live across the street from the seminary. A priori, however, one would guess that the number of home buyers with reasons as atypical as these would be small indeed because in all except the rarest of cases houses in all-white areas would meet the requirements, desires, and preferences of home purchasers.

Most of the purchasers gave commonplace reasons for their choice of residence. Virtually all of the purchasers listed such factors as convenience to work, school, friends, and relatives, or they gave general responses such as "I am accustomed to the neighborhood and I like to live here" (table 9). Several purchasers men-

TABLE 9

REASONS GIVEN FOR CHOICE OF AREA BY WHITE PURCHASERS
AND RENTERS IN THE STUDY AREAS, 1955

Reason for Choice	Purchasers		Renters	
	Number	Percent	Number	Percent
Convenience of neighborhood	65	33.5	38	38.0
Business and employment	34	17.5	21	21.0
Family and friends	32	16.5	19	19.0
Suitability of house	41	21.1	13	13.0
Special reasons	6	3.1	5	5.0
Ethnic reasons	5	2.6	. . .	. . .
No answers and don't know	11	5.7	4	4.0
Total	194	100.0	100	100.0

tioned that the price of the house was attractive. Since it can be assumed that none of the purchases would have been made if the price were not satisfactory, the relative infrequency with which this response appears perhaps indicates that few unusual bargains were to be had.

The lack of compelling reason is less astonishing than the fact that at least three-fourths of the respondents did not bother to look for a house in any other area and that an additional 5 percent, though they did look elsewhere, considered the racially mixed area to be their first choice (table 10). Even those white home buyers (20 percent of total) who looked for a house in all-white areas were, according to their responses, only in rare cases forced by circumstances to accept a racially mixed area. In general, the respondents said they confined their search for a house to the mixed area because many of them already lived or worked in

TABLE 10
ALTERNATIVE AREAS CONSIDERED BY WHITE PURCHASERS
AND RENTERS IN THE STUDY AREAS, 1955

Areas considered	Purchasers		Renters	
	Number	Percent	Number	Percent
No other areas	149	76.8	79	79.0
Anywhere else in Philadelphia	14	7.2	6	6.0
Suburbs	19	9.8	13	13.0
Others	9	4.6	...	...
No answer and don't know	3	1.6	2	2.0
Total	194	100.0	100	100.0

the area and their information about available houses was greater than for other areas.

The mundane character of the reasons given for the residential choice led us to wonder whether the purchasers found it difficult to express the hierarchical importance which they attached to the factors determining their residential location. The process of purchasing a home is not completely a rational one. Some factors such as those which circumscribe the residential location of a family—its financial position and the journey to work of its major wage earner—may be clearly perceived; other factors such as those which determine the final choice—familiarity with and attachment to a neighborhood, proximity to friends and relatives, special features of a house, and other predilections or aversions—may be only vaguely felt and rarely verbalized. Hence, in order to detect some of the motives of white purchasers for living in racially mixed areas, the analyst must resort to other data. The following subsections will discuss, therefore, several factors which seem pertinent as indicators of reason for the specific locational choice of the home buyers.

Journey to work of major wage earner.—The journey to work of the head of the household circumscribes, though it does not pinpoint, the residential location of a family. Various studies have shown that the preponderant demand for housing in any area comes from those households in which the major wage earner's place of work is located within a reasonable time-distance from the place of residence. While some Philadelphians do not mind commuting long distances, the overwhelming majority reside in an area within forty minutes of their place of employment.

In all, convenience to business and employment were given as reasons for moving to the racially mixed areas by approximately 15 percent of the respondents. Roughly one-half of the household heads worked in the general area in which they resided or in nearby Center City, suggesting that even for those who did not mention journey to work, convenience to place of employment may have been an important factor.

Home purchase alternatives.—The income of the home purchasers suggests that their housing opportunities were limited to areas in which moderately priced homes were available. With few exceptions, the white buyers could have acquired homes at the same or lower price in only about one-half of the neighborhoods of the city, and approximately 50 percent of these areas were mixed or nonwhite in composition. Some of the all-white areas were beyond reasonable commuting distance. Thus the residential choice of many of the families was indeed circumscribed, but it was by no means completely limited to mixed areas. There were a number of acceptable and, in fact, attractive alternatives that the white families could have selected had the question of racial proximity been a matter of serious concern to them.

Association with the neighborhood.—Familiarity with and attachment to the neighborhood undoubtedly played an important role in determining the choice of residential areas. Over 60 percent of the white home purchasers were residents of the area prior to the date of acquisition and 40 percent had lived in the area five years or longer (table 11). This fact suggests that there may be more significance to the response, "I am accustomed to the neighborhood and I like to live here," than appears on the surface.

TABLE 11

DISTRIBUTION OF HOUSEHOLDS BY PERIOD OF ENTRANCE IN NEIGHBORHOOD
OF PURCHASE FOR WHITE PURCHASERS IN THE STUDY AREAS, 1955

Year of initial residence	Number	Percent
1955	74	38.2
1950 to 1954	44	22.7
1945 to 1949	15	7.7
1940 to 1944	8	4.1
Prior to 1940	52	26.8
No answer	1	.5
Total	194	100.0

When a respondent who is an immigrant or the child of an immigrant states that he is attracted to the neighborhood because of his desire to be near his friends and relatives, he may, in fact, be referring to a group atmosphere with which he especially wishes to associate and be identified. There is a strong likelihood that each of the areas was associated in the minds of many purchasers with its previous national or religious character rather than with its changing racial composition. That is, though an Italian may know Tasker now has many Negroes, perhaps he still thinks of it as Italian and is attracted to the area because there are a reassuring number of Italian institutions at hand. For similar reasons, perhaps the Jewish purchaser, native or immigrant, wants to live in Strawberry Mansion or a section of West Philadelphia even though he knows of its many Negroes.

RACIAL COMPOSITION OF NEIGHBORHOOD OF PREVIOUS RESIDENCE

Up to this point no mention has been made of the racial composition of the neighborhoods from which white purchasers in mixed areas came. If these purchasers previously resided in areas that had heavier concentrations of Negro population, then the move to the mixed study areas may have been motivated by a desire to live in a neighborhood that had a higher proportion of white persons. Thus, these families may not have left the previous area because of the presence of Negroes, but rather because of their high proportion in the neighborhood.

To pursue this question, white purchasers in West Philadelphia were classified into two distinct groups: those who had moved within the study area and those who came from neighborhoods outside of the study area. Virtually all of the families in the first group had left the mixed zone and had moved to houses in the white zone which were located at least four blocks to the south of their former residence. The second group accounted for almost all of the white purchasers in the mixed zone, two-thirds of whom had previously lived in white areas (table 12).

The West Philadelphians who moved within the area, and those who moved from mixed neighborhoods outside of West Philadelphia to the mixed section of that area, may have done so

TABLE 12

PERCENT DISTRIBUTION OF WHITE PURCHASERS BY RACIAL COMPOSITION OF AREAS
OF PREVIOUS AND PRESENT RESIDENCE, WEST PHILADELPHIA, 1955

Previous area	Present area		Total
	White	Mixed	
White	27	40	67
Mixed	12	21	33
Total	39	61	100

in an attempt to find a neighborhood with a lower proportion of Negro population. But this surely cannot be the case for those families who lived in white areas before moving to West Philadelphia and then purchased a home in the mixed section of that area. This group was either indifferent to the racial composition of the destination area or felt that the positive features overbalanced any limitation introduced by the mixed character of the population.

In summary, the motivations of the white buyers suggest some of the barriers to and supports of interracial neighborhoods. The buyers were strongly attracted to the mixed areas in which they acquired homes. More than three-quarters did not look for a house in any other neighborhood, yet they gave no unusual or unique reasons for their purchase. House price and place of employment were considerations that strongly affected the residential choice of the buyers as they do in any other sector of the housing market. A desire to live in an area with a lower proportion of Negroes seems to have been a factor in the moving decision of some of the families. Most important, however, was the fact that many of the buyers were already either long-time residents of or intimately associated with the general area in which they located. The concentration of religious and cultural groups present in the mixed areas strengthened these ties and served as an important attractive force for many of the white purchasers.

AWARENESS AND ATTITUDES OF WHITE PURCHASERS

In order to interpret the reasons for home purchase in racially mixed areas, it is necessary to know whether white families knew about Negro occupancy in their neighborhoods and what their attitudes toward Negro residential proximity were.[9] One set of questions therefore was devoted to determining the extent of the purchasers' knowledge of Negro occupancy of the area and of Negro migration into the area. Another set of questions was designed to elicit directly the respondents' attitudes toward Negro residential proximity. The following subsections discuss these two problems—awareness of the presence of Negroes and attitudes toward Negro residential proximity.

Awareness of the presence of Negroes.—Most of the respondents were long-time residents of Philadelphia. At the time of the interview, almost 75 percent had lived in the city or metropolitan area for more than fifteen years and another 7 percent had lived there at least five years, whereas only 4 percent had moved to Philadelphia during 1955, the year in which they bought a house in one of the study areas. Similarly, as previously noted, almost 40 percent of all respondents had lived in the neighborhood into which they purchased for more than five years. In fact, more than one-fourth had moved to the neighborhood as they defined it before 1940 (see table 11). The length of residence of the respondents in Philadelphia, but particularly in the neighborhood, makes it appear unlikely that more than a handful blundered into an area that they ordinarily would not have chosen because of lack of time or opportunity to learn about its racial composition.

Although most of the white purchasers presumably did not have the newcomer's lack of knowledge of the general area, they may not have been aware of Negro occupancy in the locale into which they purchased, either because of indifference to their neighbors or because the neighborhood had begun to change so recently that knowledge was difficult to obtain. Several questions were designed, therefore, to determine directly the extent of the respondents' knowledge. Slightly less than three-fourths of the respondents were aware of the presence of Negroes in their neigh-

---

[9] The reader's attention is drawn to the fact that individual concepts of "neighborhood" often show wide differences. What one respondent called "the neighborhood" may exclude some blocks considered a part of "the neighborhood" by another respondent. Similarly, any one person may think of a neighborhood as consisting of different area dimensions when talking in different contexts.

borhoods at the time of the interview.[10] This fact was indicated by their answers to questions concerning sources of dissatisfaction with the neighborhood or by their answer to the question, "Are there any people in the neighborhood whose race or religion is different from yours? Who are they?" (table 13).

TABLE 13

AWARENESS OF NEGROES IN NEIGHBORHOOD BY WHITE PURCHASERS
AT THE TIME OF INTERVIEW, 1956

Degree of awareness	Number	Percent
Aware	139	71.7
Uncertain (presumably unaware)	22	11.3
Unaware	2	1.0
No answer	31	16.0
Total	194	100.0

In other words, slightly more than one-fourth of the respondents either stated that they did not know whether there were any people in their neighborhood whose race differed from theirs or would give no answer at all. We may now ask, were these people in full possession of the facts regarding the racial composition of their neighborhood, but unwilling to commit themselves; or were they persons who felt that they lacked the knowledge required to answer the questions? That the second of these possibilities is more likely is illustrated by a comparison of these responses by study area. A larger proportion of respondents in the West Philadelphia area than in the other areas claimed uncertainty or did not reply to the question—34 percent as against 18 percent for respondents in other areas. It may be recalled that West Philadelphia is an area of fast change with respect to racial composition and that until recently many parts of it had a very low proportion of Negro residents—less than 2 percent. Presumably respondents living in the remaining all-white blocks or in blocks to which a Negro family had moved only very recently may have been uncertain about the racial composition of their neighborhood, or they may have thought of it as consisting of only all-white blocks, or they may have been uncertain as to which houses, street fronts, and/or blocks constituted their neighborhood. It is probable also that a small proportion of the "no answer" group knew but chose not to

---

[10] These respondents will be referred to as the "aware-group."

TABLE 14
Point of Awareness of Negroes in Neighborhood by Length of Residence in Neighborhood, West Philadelphia White Purchasers, 1955

Years of residence	Before purchase		After purchase		Negro entry after purchase		No answer		Total	
	Number	Percent	Number	Percent	Number	Percent	Number	Percent	Number	Percent
Less than 1	17	51.5	16	48.5	...	...	...	...	33	100.0
1–5.9	7	30.4	13	56.5	2	8.7	1	4.4	23	100.0
6–15.9	3	37.5	3	37.5	2	25.0	...	...	8	100.0
16 and over	12	63.2	6	31.6	1	5.2	...	...	19	100.0
Total	39	47.0	38	45.8	5	6.0	1	1.2	83	100.0

respond in order to avoid becoming involved in racial questions.

After determining the proportion of the purchasing families who were in full possession of information regarding the racial composition of the area into which they purchased at the time of the interview, it was necessary to establish whether this information was acquired before or after the purchase of the home. When a direct question using the term "Negro" was put to the respondents, approximately three-fifths of the "awares" stated that they had known of the fact that Negroes lived in the neighborhood before they purchased their homes. About one-third stated that they found out that Negroes lived in the neighborhood after they bought their homes (table 14). If these respondents are regarded as "unaware" because they were not aware of the presence of Negro residents in the neighborhood at the time of purchase, the "unaware" and "presumably unaware" group becomes very large totaling almost one-half of all respondents who answered the question.

Another possible determinant of awareness suggested by the pattern of responses to the questionnaire is the proximity of Negro neighbors to the respondent. It is probable that a single Negro family located a block or two from a respondent's residence might not have come to his attention. Evidence from the questionnaire suggests that the more recent the racial change and the further removed from the center of change the respondents are, the less aware they seem to be of the transition process. This is illustrated in the case of West Philadelphia, where 73 percent of the respondents in the mixed zone were aware of Negroes in the locality at the time of interview, compared with only 63 percent of the whites who purchased in the white zone. It is, of course, possible that some of the buyers in the white zone may have adopted as their definition of "neighborhood" an area which excluded the zone of Negro penetration to the north, since twenty-five of the fifty-seven buyers interviewed in the white zone bought two or more blocks away from the mixed area. However, several of the blocks in the white area were mixed at the time of the inquiry and none of the fifty-seven buyers were more than two blocks away from a mixed block.

Many real estate agents maintain that they endeavor to make

prospective buyers aware of the prevailing racial characteristics and racial trends in the neighborhood, and that, for example, they direct prospective white buyers away from mixed blocks.[11] This policy if universally observed should make most buyers fully aware of the racial character of the area into which they intend to move, since negotiations with brokers occur in almost all cases before a purchase agreement is reached. It is unlikely, however, that real estate agents who enter the scene at the last stages of negotiation would attempt to dissuade prospective buyers. Only seven of the twenty-two West Philadelphia respondents who bought in the mixed zone and who learned about their home through a real estate agent were aware of Negroes in the neighborhood before moving; six specifically stated that they learned after moving, one stated that he moved in before Negroes, and eight fell into the "no awareness" category. This suggests either that all real estate agents operating in the transitional area do not inform their white clients or that the process of transition took place before the negotiations were finished.

A final factor governing awareness may be the degree of ethnic or social homogeneity in the neighborhood. In a highly integrated neighborhood where friendships spread over a wide area and residents are bound together by ethnic, religious, cultural, or organizational ties, communication may be greater than in an area in which local residents have divergent social backgrounds and seek their community life outside the neighborhood. The design of the questionnaire did not permit a determination of the extent, if any, to which the presence or absence of integrated community life was a contributing factor to the degree of awareness which new buyers had of Negro in-migration.

Attitudes toward Negro occupancy.—One of the most interesting facts to emerge from this study was that a large proportion of white families who purchased homes in mixed areas in 1955 had strong objections to the presence of Negroes in the immediate vicinity, and if any were motivated by a desire to foster harmonious race relations in mixed areas, they were indeed few in num-

---

[11] Interviews with real estate agents; also Marketers' Research Service, Inc., *Survey of Housing Market Practices of Builders, Brokers and Mortgage Lenders in the Philadelphia Urban Area* (Philadelphia, October, 1955).

ber. The data presented in this subsection describe the distribution
of racial attitudes found among white purchasers, the misgivings
of buyers about the racial composition of the neighborhood, and
their feelings about proximity to Negro neighbors.[12] In addition,
some attempt has been made to examine the relationship between
expressed or implied attitudes and the behavior of the respondents. Data on attitudes were secured by means of two sets of
questions. In the first, an attempt was made to elicit a general
expression of feeling regarding the residence of Negroes in the
area; in the second, direct questions were addressed to the respondent regarding his attitude toward varying degrees of residential proximity to Negroes.

The first general question designed to elicit an attitudinal response was phrased as follows: "Did you find out anything which
made you doubt your choice of house or neighborhood before you
moved here?" If the respondent replied "yes," he was asked:
"What were these doubts?" Few (13 percent) of the total respondents stated that they had any misgivings prior to their purchase. Two-thirds of this group (16 persons) volunteered that the
presence of Negroes led them to question the wisdom of buying
a home in the area. This number represents 20 percent of the respondents who admitted that they were aware of the presence of
Negroes in the area prior to their purchase. In other words, 80
percent of those who did know that Negroes lived in the area had
no expressed misgivings at all. The respondents were then asked,
"Now that you have lived here for a while, are you in any way
dissatisfied with the neighborhood?" Of the 139 respondents who
stated they were aware of Negroes in the area at the time of the
interview, 43, or 31 percent, cited this fact as a reason for current
dissatisfaction. Only four of the sixteen persons who had misgivings prior to purchase were in this group; the remaining twelve
presumably found their apprehensions to be groundless.

The bulk of respondents who voiced dissatisfaction were persons who did not learn until after their purchase that Negroes re-

---

[12] The limited size of the sample of respondents made it impossible to obtain
satisfactory data on the association between attitudes toward residential proximity
to Negroes and the characteristics of white purchasers. From the cross tabulations
in general it appeared that differences between study areas were much greater than
differences within these areas.

sided in the area. These families did not have the opportunity to decide whether they wished to live in a mixed area, and they were therefore asked whether they intended to leave the neighborhood because of the presence of Negroes.

Twenty or close to one-third of the fifty-nine respondents in this group, stated that they desired to leave the neighborhood. Only six respondents stated that they were actively seeking a new place to live, and three out of the six reported that they still would want to leave the neighborhood even if all the residents were white. Thus, only three of the families who did not face the issue of Negro residence in the area prior to their purchase of a dwelling reported that they were making plans to leave because of the mixed character of the area.

The white families who indicated awareness of the presence of Negroes in the neighborhood were asked an additional question, "How do you feel about owning a home in the same neighborhood with Negroes? On the same block? Next door?" The response to this series of questions showed that the degree of hypothetical proximity was distinctly correlated with the proportion of positive or negative references. Sixty percent of the respondents expressed approval or indifference to the residence of Negroes in the neighborhood, 40 percent to residence on the same block, and 31 percent to residence in an adjacent house (table 15). Only 4 percent of the respondents voiced strong disapproval of Negro residence in the neighborhood but 31 percent expressed the same intensity of feeling about Negro residence next door. There was little variation in the proportion of respondents who expressed moderate disapproval to each of the three suggested situations.

TABLE 15

PERCENT DISTRIBUTION OF ATTITUDES OF WHITE HOME PURCHASERS IN MIXED AREAS TOWARD VARYING DEGREES OF HYPOTHETICAL PROXIMITY TO NEGRO RESIDENTS

Attitude	Degree of proximity		
	Same neighborhood	Same block	Next door
Approval or indifference	60	40	31
Moderate disapproval	34	41	30
Strong disapproval	4	14	31
No answer and don't know	2	5	8
Total	100	100	100

Further analysis of the interviews in West Philadelphia was undertaken to see if there was any relationship between attitude of the purchaser and the racial characteristics of the zone in which the purchase was made. It was found that a higher proportion of the families who had purchased into the mixed zone either approved or were indifferent to the residence of Negroes at each level of proximity. Thus, three-fourths of the white purchasers in the mixed zone expressed approval or indifference to the residence of Negroes in the same neighborhood, while only a little more than one-half in the white zone expressed approval. Fifty-five percent in the mixed zone expressed approval of Negro residence on the same block, as against 46 percent in the white zone who re-

TABLE 16

PERCENT DISTRIBUTION OF ATTITUDES OF WHITE HOME PURCHASERS
IN WEST PHILADELPHIA TOWARD VARYING DEGREES OF HYPOTHETICAL PROXIMITY
TO NEGRO RESIDENTS, BY ZONE OF PURCHASE

| Attitude | Racial zone and degree of proximity | | | | | |
| | Same neighborhood | | Same block | | Next door | |
	Mixed zone	White zone	Mixed zone	White zone	Mixed zone	White zone
Approval or indifference	73	53	55	46	46	38
Moderate disapproval	23	41	33	39	26	31
Strong disapproval	4	6	12	15	28	31
Total	100	100	100	100	100	100

vealed this attitude. Similarly, 46 percent of the white residents in the mixed zones said they were willing to accept Negroes as next door neighbors, while only 38 percent of the respondents in the white zones made such statements (table 16).

THE UNREALIZED POTENTIAL

In summary, there appears to have been a fairly close correspondence between attitudes and behavior on the part of the white families who purchased homes in the study areas. As would be expected, acquisitions were confined largely to families who at the time of their purchase did not disapprove of living in mixed neighborhoods (table 17). The experience in these study areas, however, does not necessarily imply that there need be the same correspondence between attitudes and behavior in mixed neighborhoods generally. There may be a large number of individuals who hold negative views on the subject but who probably could have been drawn to these areas had the houses or surroundings been more attractive in any of a variety of ways.

TABLE 17

ATTITUDE OF WHITE PURCHASERS TOWARD NEGROES LIVING IN SAME
NEIGHBORHOOD BY POINT OF AWARENESS

Point of awareness	Approval or indifference		Disapproval		Strong disapproval		Total	
	No.	Pct.	No.	Pct.	No.	Pct.	No.	Pct.
Before purchase	59	75.6	18	23.1	1	1.3	78	100.0
After purchase	20	44.4	21	46.7	4	8.9	45	100.0
Negroes came after purchase	3	27.3	8	72.7	0	...	11	100.0
Total	82	61.2	47	35.1	5	3.7	134ª	100.0

ªFive respondents did not express attitudes.

More important, perhaps, is the fact that many families with positive or neutral views did not purchase homes in these areas. It is within this group that the disparity between attitudes and behavior is crucial. This sector of the population has been growing at a steady pace in recent years, but the demand for homes in racially mixed areas on the part of white families has not expanded nearly so fast. Thus, there is an increasing potential demand that is not being realized because significant factors aside from prejudice lead potential home buyers to acquire homes in other than mixed neighborhoods. Some of these factors and their implications are explored in the next chapter.

IV

Negro Proximity and Proportion: Strategic Factors in Neighborhood Stability

It is generally recognized that white demand is the single most important factor necessary to maintain the stability of racially mixed residential areas. Without white buyers no area entered by Negroes can permanently preserve its interracial character. White owners may hasten the transition process by fleeing, or they may retard it by accepting the Negro entrants as they would any other new neighbors. In the course of time, however, every home occupied by a white family will be put up for sale and, unless white buyers can be found, all will be sold to nonwhites. The transition may take a year or it may take a decade, but without white buyers it will occur eventually.

The apparent drop of white demand in the study areas has been observed in most mixed neighborhoods throughout the country. The scarcity of white purchases in racially changing neighborhoods is frequently interpreted as an indication of widespread, deep-seated prejudices, whereas actually it reflects widespread discrimination stemming from prejudices of unknown depth.[1] A given level of prejudice may be translated into a variety of discriminatory or nondiscriminatory actions depending on the

---

[1] For an excellent discussion of the difference between prejudice and discrimination see Robert K. Merton, "Discrimination and the American Creed," in R. M. MacIver (ed.), *Discrimination and National Welfare* (New York: Harper and Brothers, 1949), p. 104.

circumstances under which a decision involving race must be made. If prejudices are strongly held by a substantial sector of the population, even very attractive interracial neighborhoods will be avoided by most white families. If, however, a large segment of the population is only slightly prejudiced, a few small changes in the institutional structure of the market or in the characteristics of changing neighborhoods or in the social and legal climate within which purchase decisions are made may result in the attraction of many white buyers to mixed areas.

Today, a number of strategic factors tend to produce decisions against purchasing in mixed neighborhoods regardless of the buyers' attitudes. Many families, for example, are able to find in all-white areas a wide selection of houses that are superior to the aging dwellings typical of most mixed neighborhoods. Other buyers avoid interracial areas because of fear of declining property values, or of crime, or of inviting the disapproval of friends and relatives.[2] Still other white families are dissuaded from purchasing homes in mixed neighborhoods by the real estate broker or by the refusal of lending institutions to finance their contemplated acquisitions.

These demand factors have been extensively explored in the literature on residential segregation and integration. Two components of demand that have received much less attention but which are critical in determining the number of both prejudiced and unprejudiced white buyers who will purchase in mixed areas are (1) the actual or expected number and proportion of Negroes in the mixed community and (2) the spatial distribution of nonwhite residences relative to the homes which white families contemplate acquiring. Because these factors are so important and since they have not been examined in detail elsewhere, this chapter is devoted to an analysis of the manner in which they affect the stability of interracial areas.

Proximity and proportion are not mutually exclusive variables. As proximity increases, proportion frequently does also. As a result, to some persons a large number of Negroes also means Negroes nearby. It is also true, however, that a person who would

---

[2] See Commission on Race and Housing, *Where Shall We Live?*, Report of the Commission (Berkeley: University of California Press, 1958), pp. 14-22.

be distressed by a large number of nonwhites in the general area might object equally to even a small number if they were in the immediate vicinity. For example, one white homeowner who was interviewed stated his objection as follows: "In the main, it is many Negroes, not Negroes per se." "I don't mind a Negro down the street, but not next door." This individual had feelings concerning both proximity and proportion, and these factors were not clearly distinguished in his mind. In the succeeding analysis, however, they have been separated in order to bring out their individual effects upon white demand.

PROXIMITY

It was observed in chapter ii that almost three-quarters of the white families purchased on or adjacent to mixed blocks and that one-fourth purchased on mixed street fronts. But less than a handful acquired a home adjacent to a Negro residence.

If it is true that whites will not purchase a home next door to nonwhites, the occupancy by a nonwhite family of a single dwelling-unit on a block (one side of the street) must inevitably result in an all-Negro block, even though it may take resident white families many years to sell their homes and move elsewhere. It may be that this is at the core of the belief that a neighborhood entered by a single Negro family will eventually become entirely nonwhite.

There are three qualifications to the generalization that a block entered by Negroes will eventually become 100 percent nonwhite. First, if the initial Negro purchaser sold his home to a white family before additional Negroes moved into the block, the all-white status of the block would be restored. This is a remote possibility because the Negro family having just arrived would probably not be ready to move voluntarily for several years. During this time, other homes would be placed on the market, and it is not unlikely that at least one or two would be sold to Negroes.

Second, the presence of rental units in the area or the conversion of some units to a rental status during the transition process helps to forestall a complete change in the ethnic composition of an area. Apartments in West Philadelphia had little difficulty in keeping white occupants even though the buildings became surrounded by an increasing proportion of nonwhite neighbors. A few of the more modern apartments reported waiting lists. In many neighborhoods, however, the number of rental units is too small to provide an effective brake to the transition process.

The third and perhaps most important qualification relates to Negro demand. If the greater market freedom for Negroes brings with it an increasing scatter of nonwhite purchasers, the day will soon come when Negroes will have bought into more blocks than the nonwhite population can fill. Transition of some of these blocks to 100 percent Negro occupancy will become impossible. In the absence of Negro purchasers white sellers in these blocks will either have to find white buyers or retain ownership of their homes indefinitely. The latter choice will probably be impossible for more than a small percentage of individuals.[3] Thus, it is clear that, although white demand is the critical factor in interracial stability, the level of Negro demand is extremely important also.

Attitudes toward residential proximity often cause white demand to dry up completely in the presence of a very low percentage of Negroes. The presence of but a single Negro resident may cause a prospective white purchaser to wonder how long it will be until the house in which he is interested is flanked by nonwhite residences, and it is probably for this reason that white demand often evaporates after the first or second Negro entrant. As a corollary, the scattering of even a small number of Negroes would be more likely to hasten transition than would a clustering of a similar or larger number. This is because in the latter instance a much smaller proportion of the market supply would be located adjacent to Negro families.

PROPORTION

Our data appear to support the view that as the proportion of Negroes in a mixed area increases, the percentage of white families who will consider the area as a place of residence declines. For many white families, doubts and apprehensions regarding status, quality of schools, property values, personal safety, and

---

[3] This might result in a price decline initially, but whether lower prices would persist is problematical. Subsequent sales to whites in the area could conceivably be at going market prices if a situation of stability were observed to exist.

social contact are all tied to the actual or anticipated number of Negroes in the neighborhood. If one or a few Negroes move to an area, very little is altered. Status is not endangered; the composition of the classroom is not influenced materially; existing social and behavior patterns continue to predominate. But as the proportion of Negro population rises, it is accompanied by a shift in the attitudes of white residents which is strengthened by changes in the social milieu. It is typical of the transition process that a large and expanding in-migrant population creates a situation in which existing institutions, formal and informal, are in danger of losing their support and face the real possibility of serious decline or disappearance. In this sense, therefore, a rising Negro population changes the actual or imagined neighborhood social setting to which white families have grown accustomed.

Although the inverse correlation between white demand and Negro population is well recognized, the rate at which white demand diminishes at given levels of Negro occupancy and under various other circumstances is not known. Such knowledge would be of inestimable value in determining what sort of interracial neighborhoods, if any, have the possibility of maintaining a stable racial mix. For this reason an attempt was made to measure this relationship in two of the study areas, West Philadelphia and Mount Airy. A calculation was first made of the relationship between white *purchases* and the proportion of Negro residents, and these results were then translated into demand schedules.

Attrition in purchases.—In order to analyze the effects of Negro population on the white market in West Philadelphia, the mixed and white sections of the area delineated earlier were subdivided into a total of five zones. The boundaries of these zones were determined by consultation with informed persons, field inspection, and reference to the data on the spatial distribution of purchases made between 1950 and 1955. The zones took the form of rather narrow, slightly curvilinear bands, adjoining one another in layer cake fashion. Moving from north to south, Zones 1 through 3 were subdivisions of the mixed section, and Zones 4 and 5 were subdivisions of the white section (figure 5). The purpose of this division was to see to what extent areas of established nonwhite occupancy, areas of change, and areas of imminent change within the study area were associated with different kinds of action in the market place. An analysis of the white and Negro purchases by zone shows the influence of racial factors on purchase decisions by white families and also indicates clearly the pattern of racial transition in the study area.

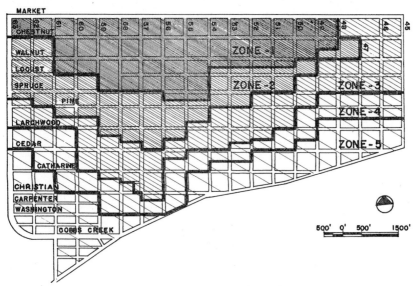

Fig. 5. Real estate submarkets, West Philadelphia study area, 1955.

In Zone 1, the area of established nonwhite residence in which approximately one-half of the blocks were mixed in 1950, Negroes constituted one-third of total population in 1955. In this zone only eight homes were acquired by white families in 1955, and this figure constituted but 4 percent of all owner-occupant purchases in the zone (table 18 and figure 6). In Zone 2, an area of later Negro entry in which the overwhelming majority of the families were white, there were 26 white purchases in 1955. This figure, however, was also only 4 percent of all owner-occupant acquisitions in the zone. Zone 3 was an area of recent Negro entry. Although the first nonwhite family had moved into the zone as early as 1953, some of the blocks were not entered until 1955, and the white population in that year was 95 percent of the total. In this zone, white demand reached significant proportions. Sixty-five of the 160 owner-occupant purchases in 1955 were by white families,

TABLE 18

WHITE AND NEGRO PURCHASES FOR OWNER-OCCUPANCY AS A PERCENT OF ONE-FAMILY STRUCTURES, BY ZONES, WEST PHILADELPHIA STUDY AREA, 1955

Zone	Percent Negro households 7/1/55	Total purchases	Owner-occupant purchases					
			Total	Negro purchases		White purchases		
				Number	Percent of one-family structures	Number	Percent of one-family structures	Percent of owner-occupant purchases
1	32	231	204	196	6.0	8	0.2	3.9
2	16	635	598	572	14.2	26	0.6	4.3
3	5	199	160	95	2.6	65	1.7	40.6
4	1	88	76	1	*	75	3.1	98.7
5	1	129	112	0	...	112	3.0	100.0
All zones	15	1,282	1,150	864	5.1	286	1.7	24.9

*Less than one-twentieth of 1 percent.

some of whom said, however, that at the time of their purchase they thought they were buying into a white area. In Zones 4 and 5 there was a fade-out of Negro demand, and in the two zones

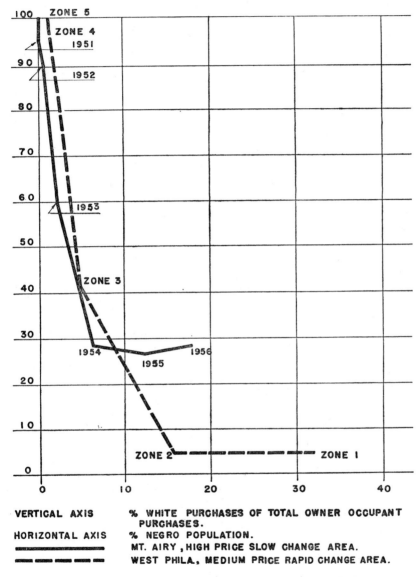

VERTICAL AXIS   % WHITE PURCHASES OF TOTAL OWNER OCCUPANT PURCHASES.

HORIZONTAL AXIS   % NEGRO POPULATION.

━━━━━━━━━━   MT. AIRY, HIGH PRICE SLOW CHANGE AREA.

━ ━ ━ ━ ━   WEST PHILA., MEDIUM PRICE RAPID CHANGE AREA.

Fig. 6. Relationship of home purchases by white families to Negro population in two areas of Philadelphia undergoing racial transition.

combined only one sale to a nonwhite family was recorded in 1955. This does not mean that the influence of Negroes in these zones was absent, for a few Negro families were in residence, and some of the white families who were interviewed in Zone 4 actually considered themselves to be in a mixed neighborhood.

In relating white purchases to Negro population in Mount Airy, a somewhat different method was employed. Since in any one year there were insufficient sales to permit a zonal analysis, the trend of white purchases was traced over a six-year period starting with the first Negro entry in the area in 1951. Despite this difference in procedure, almost precisely the same result was found in Mount Airy as in West Philadelphia. Acquisitions by white families dropped sharply when the proportion of Negroes was still extremely low (table 19 and figure 6). Here, too, white purchases

TABLE 19

WHITE AND NEGRO POPULATION AND HOME PURCHASES IN THE MIXED SECTION
OF WEST MOUNT AIRY, PHILADELPHIA, 1950–1956

Year	Dwelling units by race of occupants at beginning of year				Home purchases by race during year			
	White	Negro	Total	Percent Negro	White	Negro	Total	Percent White
1950	307	0	307	0	23	0	23	100.0
1951	307	0	307	0	16	1	17	94.1
1952	306	1	307	0.3	24	3	27	88.9
1953	303	4	307	1.3	12	8	20	60.0
1954	295	12	307	3.9	7	18	25	28.0
1955	277	30	307	9.8	6	16	22	27.3
1956	261	46	307	15.0	7	18	25	28.0

leveled off, but at a somewhat higher point than in West Philadelphia.

Attrition in demand.—Up to this point we have established only that white purchases declined as the proportion of Negroes rose. It has not been shown, however, that white demand also revealed a downward trend. Purchases and demand are not synonymous. For any demand function there could be a wide variation in the volume of purchases depending on the circumstances that prevail in a specific situation. The apparent decline of white demand for houses in mixed areas may actually have been a reflection of competition by Negroes for the available stock rather than an indication of prejudice or discrimination by white families. A simple example may serve to explain this point.

Assume there are two adjacent housing areas which are identical in every respect but one. Area A is open only to whites, while Area B has just experienced its first Negro purchase and is now regarded as a neighborhood in which Negroes may purchase homes if they wish. During the year immediately prior to Negro entry into Area B, there were 50 white purchases in each of the two areas. During the first year subsequent to Negro entry, Area A again had 50 white purchases. Area B, however, had 25 white purchases and 25 Negro purchases. Can it now be said that white demand in Area B has dropped by 50 percent? An unequivocal answer to this question cannot be given without additional information.

Once an area has been opened to Negroes, if the rate of turnover remains constant, the number of white purchases will drop if there are any Negro buyers at all. This must be true even if white buyers do not seek to discriminate. Thus, the drop in white purchases that is almost universally observed when Negroes enter a neighborhood cannot always be attributed to a shift in the white demand schedule, since the number of white acquisitions is partly a function of the level of Negro demand. Even where there is a shift in the basic schedule of white demand, it may be much less than the numerical drop in purchases would suggest. In the example above, only if there were no price shifts from one year to the next, no change in the volume of offerings, and no decrease in the elapsed time required to sell the houses, could it be said that white demand had fallen by 50 percent. For, if white demand had not fallen, the additional Negro demand would have either raised prices or at least enabled sellers to dispose of their properties more quickly.

Clearly, any attempt to measure white demand is fraught with difficulties and pitfalls because the usual statistical evidence does not lend itself readily to this type of analysis. It is possible, however, by coupling the field data with a liberal sprinkling of assumptions to bridge the gap between the rigorous theoretical requirements and the imprecision of the data. The results, nevertheless, must be accepted and interpreted with caution.[4]

---

[4] For a more extensive discussion, see William G. Grigsby, "The Residential Real Estate Market in an Area Undergoing Racial Transition" (unpublished Ph.D. dissertation, Columbia University, 1958).

Preliminary estimates of the reduction in demand were first made using figures on the volume of purchases alone, with the tentative assumption that all other factors remained constant. These estimates were then adjusted to reflect the effect which price changes may have had in reducing or increasing white purchases without causing a shift in the demand schedule. Approximately the same procedure was employed in both West Philadelphia and Mount Airy and will be described, therefore, with reference to the former area only.

A study of the transfer records revealed that a "normal" turnover rate for single family dwelling units, in West Philadelphia, prior to 1950 was about 4.8 percent. Assuming that this rate prevailed in all parts of the study area and that about 4 percent of the "absorption" was by white owner-occupants, a first approximation of the attrition in white demand can be made with reference to this figure. In Zone 1, white families purchased only 0.2 percent of the stock in 1955. This drop in acquisitions was equivalent to a decline in white demand, relative to the "norm" of previous years, of 95 percent, assuming that prices, supply, and elapsed time remained constant. In Zone 2, whites acquired 0.6 percent of the stock representing a decline in demand of 85 percent. In Zone 3, the absorption rate was 1.7 percent, reflecting an attrition of 58 percent relative to the 4 percent standard.

In Zones 4 and 5, whites absorbed 3 percent of the stock, a rate which translates into a demand decline of 25 percent, even though virtually the entire area was closed to Negroes. This conclusion, however, requires the further assumption that there was additional stock on the market in Zones 4 and 5 which whites could have absorbed had they been so inclined. In Zones 1, 2, and 3, there was of course a huge volume of additional houses which whites could have purchased, but in Zones 4 and 5, it cannot be demonstrated from the figures alone whether the low acquisition rate by whites represented a decline in demand or a reduction in the volume of houses offered for sale. Other evidence points to a decline of demand rather than of supply. A number of houses in the white zones had been up for sale for over six months and several of these had even been vacant for much of that time. Several brokers also reported that the market was slow in these zones. Thus, an estimate of a 25 percent demand reduction in Zones 4 and 5 does not seem unreasonable as a first approximation.

These estimates of demand attrition for each of the zones were, as noted earlier, computed while holding price and supply constant. In the next step of the analysis, an attempt was made to evaluate the extent to which the contraction of white purchases was the result of changes in the price level. More specifically, to what extent did the contraction in white purchases constitute a normal demand response to increased prices rather than a rejection of the area because of its existing or expected racial characteristics?

The introduction into an area of a huge Negro demand for housing, as happened in West Philadelphia, would, in the absence of an increase in the supply of houses for sale, normally result in a substantial price rise in the opened area but not elsewhere.[5] This alone would eliminate many, if not most, of the white buyers from the market. In West Philadelphia, however, Negro entry was accompanied by an expansion of the supply of houses offered for sale which tended to offset some, but not all, of the pressure toward higher prices. From 1950 to 1955, there was a greater upward movement of prices in Zones 1 and 2 than in Zones 3, 4, and 5 (see chapter vi). Moreover, the increase in the two mixed zones appeared to be in excess of that experienced in the rest of the city in recent years. This in itself would bring about some reduction in white purchases. To express this quantitatively, the original estimate of a 95 percent attrition in demand was adjusted downward on the basis of an assumption that the diminution of white demand in the mixed zones was greater than the estimated diminution in the white zones. This yielded an attrition of white demand in Zone 1 ranging from 85 to 94 percent and in Zone 2 from

---

[5] It should be pointed out that, up to a point, changes in demand could occur without any measurable variation in price or turnover, the change manifesting itself only in a shift in the average time required to dispose of properties listed for sale. A sluggish price response to alterations in demand is to be expected in housing markets because of the heterogeneity and low turnover rate of the stock and the general inexperience of buyers and sellers.

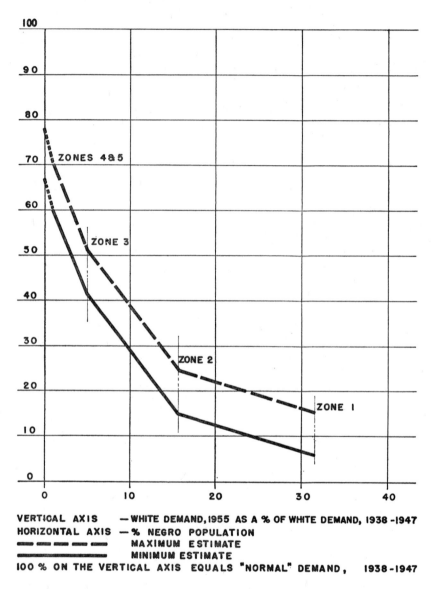

Fig. 7. Relationship of housing demand by white families to Negro population, West Philadelphia study area, 1955.

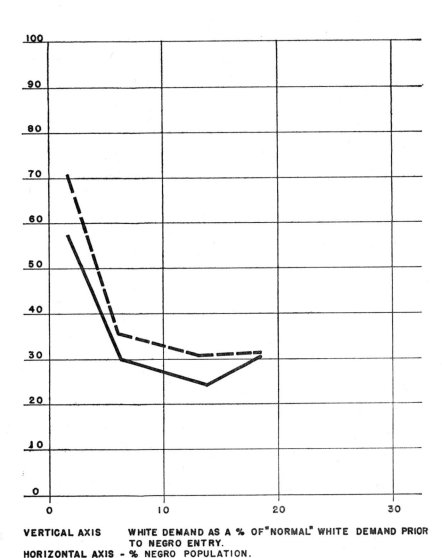

VERTICAL AXIS   WHITE DEMAND AS A % OF"NORMAL" WHITE DEMAND PRIOR
                     TO NEGRO ENTRY.
HORIZONTAL AXIS - % NEGRO POPULATION.
▬ ▬ ▬ ▬   MAXIMUM ESTIMATE
▬▬▬▬▬▬   MINIMUM ESTIMATE

Fig. 8. Relationship of housing demand by white families to Negro population, West Mount Airy, 1950–1956.

75 to 84 percent. By comparison, a demand estimate based on the proportion of white to total purchases would yield a rate of attrition of 95 percent for each of these zones.

In Zones 3, 4, and 5, the available evidence strongly suggests that between 1950 and 1955 prices rose much more gradually than in the rest of the city (see chapter vi). This disparity in price movements did not occur in the face of any known increase in the supply of houses on the market in the study area. It must, therefore, reflect a shrinkage of white demand. Furthermore, were the decline in demand inferred from the drop in white purchases alone, an understatement would result. Without lower prices in these zones, there would have been even fewer white acquisitions. It would seem reasonable to assume, therefore, that the decline in demand in Zones 4 and 5 was actually in excess of 25 percent, possibly somewhere between 30 and 35 percent. Similarly, in Zone 3 the reduction in white demand, instead of being 58 percent, was probably 60 to 65 percent.

The results of these calculations and also those for Mount Airy are depicted graphically in figures 7 and 8. The curves that emerge are of the same general shape as those in figure 6 suggesting that, barring unforeseen changes in the market, permanent interracial neighborhoods in the two study areas would be impossible, even if Negro demand were of lesser magnitude. White families would continue to acquire a decreasing percentage of the supply on the market until most of the area eventually became virtually all Negro.

Although the curves in figures 6, 7, and 8 support the popular view that predominantly Negro areas are the ultimate product of any intermingling of white and Negro residences, it would be a mistake to endow these curves with the attributes of a natural law, for the combination of circumstances that shape white demand in one neighborhood may not be present in other areas. In Philadelphia, however, white attitudes regarding mixed areas are apparently so widely and firmly held at this time that the presence of more than a few Negroes in an area outweighs all other factors which influence the purchase of homes by white families. This conclusion follows from the almost identical experience in two such dissimilar neighborhoods as Mount Airy and West Philadelphia. Mount Airy, unlike West Philadelphia, is not adjacent to an established Negro area. Moreover, both the white and non-white purchasers, as well as the resident population, are primarily of the professional and managerial class. The houses are much more expensive than those in West Philadelphia, many of them selling for over $20,000. They are, for the most part, detached and semidetached homes situated on large lots which afford considerably more privacy than do the West Philadelphia homes. Negro demand in the area has been quite moderate, and there has been a concerted effort to dissuade white families from leaving the neighborhood. The transition process has, therefore, been fairly slow. Despite these circumstances, however, the drop in both white purchases and white demand in the area was just as precipitous as in West Philadelphia. The proportion of white purchases by the end of 1956 had stabilized temporarily at a higher level than in West Philadelphia, but not at a point sufficient to stop the transition process.

CAN TRANSITION BE ARRESTED?

In view of the preceding analysis, must we conclude that an area is inevitably forced to become entirely occupied by nonwhites once Negroes have entered? If white demand is drastically reduced by the entry of a few Negroes, will this make more of the market supply available to potential nonwhite purchasers and this, in turn, reduce white demand still further until it reaches zero? There is no unequivocal answer to this question, for the outcome depends entirely on the particular circumstances surrounding the transition process. Whether stability can be achieved depends on a host of forces which can be subsumed under two categories: (a) the ratio of Negro demand to total demand before allowance is made for the effect of discrimination on white demand and (b) the extent to which various proportions of Negroes will reduce white demand.

For example, assume that in a given area 10 percent of the demand for homes is accounted for by nonwhites. Suppose also that in a mixed section of that area the effect of the presence of Negroes on white demand for housing in any price range could be described by line A, figure 9. According to this relationship which, it must be emphasized, is not empirically derived, if 10 percent of the population were Negro, white demand would be reduced by one-fourth; if 20 percent of the residents were nonwhite, white demand would be reduced by one-half; and if 40 percent of the population were nonwhite, white demand would fall to zero. Assume further that a field survey of population has just been con-

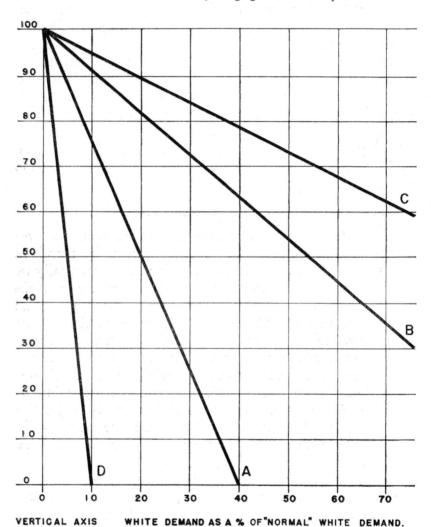

VERTICAL AXIS   WHITE DEMAND AS A % OF "NORMAL" WHITE DEMAND.
HORIZONTAL AXIS   % NEGRO POPULATION.

Fig. 9 Discrimination-demand lines.

ducted and the announced results show that the Negro population is 20 percent of total. In these circumstances, what would be the likelihood that the area would maintain a stable racial mix?

White demand in the face of 20 percent Negro occupancy would be reduced from 90 to 45 and total demand would be correspondingly reduced from 100 to 55. Nonwhite demand would, of course, remain the same. Although white demand is reduced by 50 percent, nonwhite demand, which originally was 10 percent of total at this price level, is now only 18 percent of total. Under the circumstances stipulated above, market forces will keep this percentage from rising. If no more than 80 percent of the sellers are white, the racial mixture of the area should be permanently assured, since the postulated level of white demand for houses in mixed areas with this proportion of Negro occupancy is sufficient to keep the percentage from rising.

The potential for instability may be seen by imagining a situation in which Negro demand is 16 percent of total. White demand would decline by 50 percent as before, and this would raise the initial proportion of Negro purchases to almost 30 percent of total. But it can be seen that this proportion of Negroes would reduce subsequent white demand by 70 percent. When the houses are resold, as they eventually will be, white demand will drop to 30 percent of its original level and to 60 percent of total purchases. Forty percent of the houses therefore would be transferred to Negroes. This, according to line A, would reduce white demand to zero so that when the houses were resold again, they all would be transferred to Negroes. Thus, a stable racial mix would not be achieved until the area became all Negro.

It is by now clear that in the relationship described by line A the racial mix in the examples above was determined by the ratio of Negro demand to total demand. Interracial residential stability was possible where the proportion of Negro demand to total demand was small, but was impossible where Negro demand was relatively more substantial.

It is equally clear that the range of racial proportions within which permanent interracial neighborhoods may be achieved without manipulation of the market structure is also a function of the slope of the white discrimination-demand line. Thus, line B in figure 9 shows a much more gradual slackening of white demand in the face of an increasing proportion of Negroes and therefore implies a much wider range of conditions within which stability is possible. Line C implies an even wider range. In fact, in situations represented by line C, there would be some white demand for houses in areas of 100 percent nonwhite occupancy. On the other hand, line D, which could almost be used to depict the functional relationship actually observed in West Philadelphia and Mount Airy, implies a much more narrow range within which stability can be achieved.

THE ROLE OF EXPECTATIONS

In contemplating home purchase in a transitional area, white families may attach more importance to the probable future composition of the neighborhood than to its current racial proportions. Thus, although white demand has been expressed as a function of the actual Negro population in West Philadelphia and Mount Airy, the behavior of white buyers may have been more closely related to the anticipated size of the Negro population. It is difficult to believe that white purchasers, other than the most prejudiced, would be deterred by the presence of a few Negro families unless they expected them to be joined by others. The question is raised, therefore, whether the expectation by whites of a predominantly nonwhite neighborhood may be the most crucial factor in establishing the racial composition of the area.[6] Or, are objective circumstances so determining that it is impossible for anticipations to have any permanent effect?

Regardless of the predictions that whites make, there are some circumstances in which permanent interracial neighborhoods are impossible. In the previous illustration, for example, a mixed neighborhood was impossible where Negro demand was 16 percent of total and no assumption by whites regarding the eventual racial mix would have altered this fact. There are many situations, however, in which the level of Negro demand and the shape of

---

[6] For a discussion of the manner in which expectations of an event may cause that event to occur, see Robert K. Merton, "The Self-fulfilling Prophecy," *The Antioch Review*, VIII, no. 2 (Summer, 1948). See also, Eleanor P. Wolf, "The Invasion-Succession Sequence as a Self-fulfilling Prophecy," *The Journal of Social Issues*, XIII, no. 4 (1957).

the white discrimination-demand line are such that interracial neighborhoods do become possible. In these situations, the expectations of whites are crucial in determining whether interracial projects and interracial neighborhoods can maintain a stable mixture of whites and Negroes.

To illustrate, in the example above where Negro demand was 10 percent of total, stability was possible only because white buyers acted on the assumption that the announced nonwhite population would persist at no more than 20 percent. If white buyers had concluded that the eventual proportion of Negroes in the area would rise to 50 percent, there would have been no sales to whites at all. No amount of price reductions and no amount of waiting would have changed the situation and the area in time would have become all Negro.

The importance of anticipation is by now apparent. The white discrimination-demand line for buyers in a given area may have a gradual slope, as does line B, but if the presently prevailing view among buyers is that the entry of Negroes into an area has only one inevitable consequence, then the discrimination-demand line might just as well have the slope of line D, for in either case white demand would be zero. To generate any demand by whites for houses in mixed sections under these circumstances would require positive guarantees that a given racial mix will not change in the future. It is doubtful whether such assurances could be provided, unless the entire area involved were permanently under the effective control of a single individual or group. Although this is not possible in existing neighborhoods, a small group of privately financed new developments in various parts of the country have been able to carry forth such a policy successfully.[7]

THE PROSPECT FOR CHANGE

We have seen that the likelihood of stability of racially mixed areas is largely a function of the attrition of white demand in the face of various levels of Negro occupancy. In the two areas in

---

[7] See Eunice and George Grier, *Privately Developed Interracial Housing* (Berkeley: University of California Press, 1960); see also by the same authors, "Buyers of Interracial Housing: A Study of the Market for Concord Park," Institute for Urban Studies, University of Pennsylvania, January, 1957.

Philadelphia for which this calculation was made, an immediate and sharp decline accompanied the early stages of nonwhite in-migration and home purchases. Some of the decline was no doubt a reflection of racial prejudices on the part of white buyers. But it must also be remembered that these measurements were made during a particular period of Philadelphia's history. In the decade between the end of the war and 1955, a surge of Negro housing demand occurred as a result of massive in-migration from the South, rising incomes, liberal financing, and abolition of restrictive covenants. This setting served to support a self-fulfilling prophecy. Potential white purchasers witnessing the beginning of racial transition anticipated a rapid and pervasive spread of Negro population in these sections. They therefore assumed that this phenomenon was an inevitable concomitant of Negro entry. Thus, potential purchasers who may not have been prejudiced, but who were reluctant to move into a predominantly Negro area, withdrew from the mixed-area market. By operating in this fashion they guaranteed the realization of that which they predicted.

In recent years there has been a vitiation of some of the factors that were responsible for the rapid and virtually complete transition of most areas entered by Negroes. The backlog of demand has been largely satisfied; in-migration has dropped sharply; and many of the market barriers have been lowered. Under these circumstances it is not likely that the transition pattern of the postwar decade will persist. As potential purchasers observe mixed areas that have maintained this balance over a longer period of time, the anticipation of inundation will decline. Under such circumstances there is every reason to expect that the demand curves presented in this chapter will be altered materially and that fewer white purchasers will be deterred from purchasing in mixed neighborhoods.

V

The First Negro Family: A Strategic
Aspect of Nonwhite Demand

In preceding chapters a general view has been presented of the dimension and characteristics of nonwhite demand for housing within the study area and also in Philadelphia as a whole. This demand, because of still relatively low nonwhite incomes and also because of discrimination in the new construction market, has been restricted almost exclusively to units in the standing stock. Moreover, since the receptivity of whites to Negro neighbors has varied from neighborhood to neighborhood, nonwhite demand for additional housing has tended to focus at the points of least resistance.

With due allowance for the effects of discrimination, the size of the Negro sector of the market, like the white sector, is primarily a function of population, income, family size, and the availability of mortgage credit. There may be, it is true, some attrition of nonwhite purchasers in a mixed situation if the proportion of Negroes in the neighborhood is quite low and if satisfactory housing alternatives in Negro sections are available, but this view has never been formally examined. On the whole, however, it does not appear that nonwhite demand for interracial housing need be analyzed to the same extent and depth as was white demand.

There are, nevertheless, a small number of nonwhite demanders who are of particular importance in changing areas. They are the Negroes who first enter all-white neighborhoods and who, by the seemingly simple fact of their purchase, both start the transition of the area and create a new supply of housing available to non-whites.

The way of the first Negro entrant or "block breaker,"[1] as he is more frequently called, is not an easy one either before or after the purchase. He is faced first with the prospect of entering an all-white neighborhood where his minimum difficulty may be a period of social isolation until another Negro family arrives and where the maximum penalty may include damage to his property and even physical harm to himself, wife, or children.[2]

A Negro willing to face these risks has still to find a white owner who will sell to him. In his search he is likely to obtain little assistance from the average real estate office. Few brokers assist in the breaking of blocks, and those who do have been characterized as unscrupulous operators bent only upon extracting excessive, perhaps even illicit, payments from an activity which is detrimental to most of the community. For example, the member of a respected real estate firm stated that his organization might consider "breaking" a block adjacent to one that was already mixed if the rate of Negro expansion were rapid, but that the firm would never make a sale which would put a Negro family two or more blocks inside a white area. Even should the real estate brokers be coöperative, however, sellers in the neighborhood in which the Negro family desires to live may not be "ready and willing" when confronted with a Negro buyer. For the seller, too, faces risks of social ostracism or physical harm if he transfers title to a Negro.[3] According to a number of real estate operators, it

---

[1] The appellation is also sometimes used to describe the lender who finances the first Negro purchase or the real estate broker who arranges the deal. It should be noted that the word "block" as used in this expression usually refers to the street front (the two facing sides of the street) and not to the rectangular block as a whole.

[2] For more information on the difficulties faced by Negroes who move into white neighborhoods, see Henry G. Stetler, *Racial Integration in Private Residential Neighborhoods in Connecticut* (Hartford: State of Connecticut Commission on Civil Rights, 1957), chap. iii. See also Hannah Lees, "Not Wanted," *The Atlantic Monthly*, January, 1956, pp. 59-63; also the annual reports of the Commission on Human Relations, City of Philadelphia.

[3] To illustrate, a member of the staff of the Philadelphia Police Commissioner reported that one lady who sold her home to a Negro in 1955 was, after having been threatened by her neighbors, forced to live in virtual hiding for a number of months and was convoyed to and from work by a police escort.

is the seller, not the broker, who most frequently refuses to deal with a nonwhite purchaser.

If the Negro buyer finally locates a seller who wants to do business with him, he may find that this also is not enough. A civic improvement association may suddenly emerge and offer a higher price for the house. Or, as is frequently said to occur, the Negro learns that his credit rating is not quite acceptable to mortgage lenders. Illustrative of this possibility is the statement of an officer of one of the leading Philadelphia lending institutions that, as a matter of principle and in the interests of good business, his firm never financed a sale which would break a block or place a Negro next door to one of the bank's depositors.

The Negroes who are able to circumvent or overcome all these difficulties must be, it would seem, individuals of rare talents and great personal fortitude. Yet, little is known about them, for information on the first Negro families to enter white blocks has never been systematically assembled. In order to fill part of this gap in our knowledge about mixed areas, a group of "first" families in West Philadelphia were identified and interviewed.

IDENTIFICATION OF FIRST NEGRO ENTRANTS

The identification of the Negro families who were the first nonwhites to enter their street front involved two steps: first, approximately seventy street fronts were selected in which it appeared that the first sale to a Negro family had occurred in 1955. Then a Negro interviewer was sent to each of the 1955 Negro purchasers on these blocks to determine their precise dates of acquisition and occupancy.

The Negro interviewer reported that many families seemed eager to claim the distinction of being first on the block, but that by probing he was able to obtain accurate information in virtually all cases. The information received from the households was, nevertheless, verified on a sample basis by a white interviewer who spoke with informed persons in the neighborhood. The few cases in which statements conflicted were removed from further consideration.

The field investigation yielded forty-five Negro "first" families among the 1955 purchasers. The investigation also yielded seventeen first families whose acquisitions were made prior or subsequent to 1955, and five first families who were renters. Because this study is confined to 1955 sales, neither of the latter two groups were studied.

SPATIAL DISTRIBUTION OF THE PURCHASERS

Most of the street fronts of initial entry were located in Zone 3, but this was in some measure the result of prejudgment. Since it was felt that the first entrants in 1955 would be concentrated in Zone 3, a majority of the blocks selected for investigation were in this zone. There were enough observations scattered throughout the area, however, to provide some view on the pattern and pace of diffusion of the Negro population in West Philadelphia.

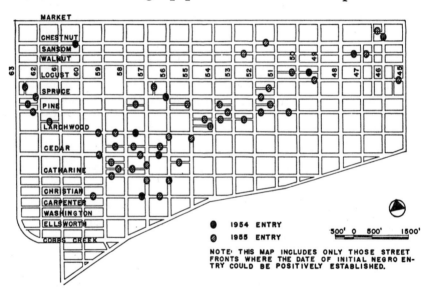

Fig. 10. White street fronts entered by Negro purchasers, West Philadelphia study area, 1954–1955.

The striking feature of the purchases was their scatter. It does not appear that the extension of the Negro community from the northern to the southern section of the area has been the gradual block by block advance usually regarded as the typical dispersion pattern. Although at least one Negro family had purchased a home located but two blocks from the southern border in 1954, some of the blocks near Market Street (the northern border) were not entered by nonwhites until 1955 and 1956 (figure 10).

FINANCIAL CHARACTERISTICS OF THE TRANSACTIONS

It will be shown in the following chapter that the purchases by Negro and white families in West Philadelphia in 1955 were similar with respect to price, ratio of price to assessed value, and sources and terms of mortgage loans. Although these findings were unexpected, it is pointed out that they were not too astonishing, because once nonwhites have entered an area, sellers, lenders, and brokers are, to some extent, forced to treat white and Negro buyers on an equal basis. There is, however, no a priori reason to anticipate equal treatment for "block breakers." It was indeed surprising therefore to find that sales to first Negro families differed very little from sales to owner-occupant families as a whole.

For all families the average purchase price was $8,310; for first families it was $8,370. Seventy-five percent of the loans made, both to all owner-occupant purchasers and to first families, carried an interest charge of 4½ percent. Further comparisons reveal additional similarities. Forty-seven percent of the first families, as compared with 57 percent of all families, received mortgage financing equal to 90 percent or more of purchase price. Local lenders financed 38 percent of the purchases by first families and 44 percent of the acquisitions by all families.

There were, to be sure, a few differences between transactions involving the first Negro entrants and those involving white buyers and, to a somewhat lesser extent, other Negro buyers. For example, one-third of the first-entrants as against one-seventh of all white and nonwhite purchasers for owner-occupancy acquired their homes from absentee owners. Twenty percent of the first families compared with only 5 percent of all buyers acquired properties which had been transferred twice in 1955. On the whole, these differences are of minor importance and this, perhaps, is the most important fact concerning them.

It is of particular interest to observe that the mortgage-lending fraternity apparently was not reluctant to break blocks in West

Philadelphia. The transactions which brought Negro families into all-white street fronts were financed by eighteen different mortgagees, of which seventeen were established lending institutions.[4] The apparent willingness of the institutions to make such loans may, however, be limited to areas that are in transition and to blocks which appear to be destined for early entry by Negroes in any event.

CHARACTERISTICS OF THE FIRST FAMILIES

Interviews with the first families revealed that, demographically, they were of higher socioeconomic status than the average Philadelphia Negro family, but that they had no characteristics which would distinguish them as a peculiar or particular group. All were married couples, two out of three of whom had children. Only one household in nine had additional adults living with the family and in every case these extra persons were close relatives. Average household size was 3.48, or approximately the same as the Philadelphia average.[5] Median family income was $4,700, considerably higher than the median both for all Negro families in Philadelphia and for Negroes who purchased homes in the city in 1955 and 1956.[6] Two-thirds of the household heads were blue-collar workers; one-sixth were white-collar employees and an equal number business or professional men. In one-third of the families there was a full-time secondary wage earner contributing to the income of the houshold. All but three of the family heads had received at least one year of high school education. Over one-half had completed high school, and five had completed one or more years of college work.

The buyers were, without exception, long-time residents of Philadelphia, all having lived in the city at least ten years.[7] In

---

[4] All were managed by whites.

[5] Average household size for Philadelphia nonwhites in 1950 was 3.55, according to the Census of Population and Housing. Calculations based on unpublished data from the U.S. Bureau of the Census, 1956 National Housing Inventory, indicate that the corresponding figure for 1956 was 3.42.

[6] Unpublished data from the 1956 National Housing Inventory show that median nonwhite family income in Philadelphia in 1956 was $3,320 and that the corresponding figure for 1955 and 1956 Negro home buyers was $3,860.

[7] By comparison, unpublished data from the 1956 National Housing Inventory show that over 85 percent of all Negro household heads in Philadelphia had resided in the metropolitan area for ten years or longer.

fact, all but a few had lived nowhere else during their adult life. One-half of them had moved to the study area from nearby neighborhoods in West Philadelphia and one-third had come from South Philadelphia. In only two instances was the previous address outside the city. Thus, these families had had the opportunity to watch developments in the housing market over many years and no doubt by the time of their purchase decision were clearly aware of the extent and nature of the risks involved.

In summary, the first families appeared to be remarkably similar to other nonwhites in the city. Although slightly higher on the socioeconomic scale than the average Philadelphia Negro family, they probably were not significantly different from the average Philadelphia Negro home buyer. If they had a more than normal desire to break a block, it probably stemmed from more than normal courage rather than a desire to make the area available to other Negro families.

PURCHASE EXPERIENCE OF THE FIRST FAMILIES

In neighborhoods where Negro entry would entail considerable trouble and risk, one would hardly anticipate finding as many as forty-five pioneering families in a single year. It would be expected, therefore, that the first families in West Philadelphia did not meet with much resistance, and this was indeed true in practically every case. All of the first families sought the services of a real estate broker and, in every instance, complete coöperation was received. Similarly, only two families said they had encountered difficulty persuading a white owner to sell to them. Relations with their new white neighbors were equally satisfactory. When asked how the whites on the block had reacted to their entry, only two Negro families described any disagreeable occurrences. Most of the respondents stated that the whites had been quite nice, but were moving out. For all but a few families, the whole experience was as simple as buying a house.

CONCLUSION

Finding so many Negro families who encountered little difficulty in entering white blocks, although an encouraging sign on the surface, has more than one implication. On the one hand, the facts suggest a relaxation of discriminatory practices in Philadelphia's housing market. At the same time, the facts could lead equally to the conclusion that by 1955, brokers, mortgage lenders, owners, and sellers alike had recognized that West Philadelphia was destined to become a mixed or predominantly nonwhite community and that it was futile to resist the inevitable.[8] Even if the latter conclusion is accepted, however, there is much encouragement to be found in the equal treatment which nearly every Negro family apparently received in its quest for the ownership of satisfactory homes in virtually all-white sections.

[8] In fact, it is conceivable that some lenders may have deliberately promoted the racial change in order to reduce pressure by Negroes for housing in all-white areas. This possibility was not explored.

VI

Financing and Prices

Although many social and demographic factors provide the setting for the racial transition of neighborhoods, the focal point of the process is to be found in the real estate market. Price levels, price trends, mortgage terms, mortgage lending policies, all have a significant impact on white and nonwhite demand and, therefore, in determining what happens to the racial characteristics of an area.

For example, if premium prices are exacted from nonwhites, many may choose to spend a larger portion of their incomes for automobiles, food, clothing, entertainment, or other items for which they can compete with white buyers on an equal basis. If nonwhites are required to make larger down payments, fewer still will be able to purchase homes in any given price class, and this will slow their rate of entry. Nonwhite entry into some areas may be stopped completely if mortgagees refuse to finance their proposed purchases in these areas. Exclusion of Negroes from some areas affects demand, prices, and rate of transition in the neighborhoods where it is possible for them to purchase a home.

On the other hand, if white owners living in sections in which racial change is impending or under way cannot get satisfactory prices for their dwellings, they may be reluctant or financially unable to leave and thereby retard the transition process. At the same time, low prices might attract white buyers who otherwise would be reluctant to purchase in mixed neighborhoods. These economic variables affecting the rate, nature, and extent of racial transition may be better understood through an analysis of the financial data.

With this goal in mind, the public record of every bona fide house sale in 1955 in each of the study areas was examined for the purpose of illuminating those aspects of the mixed area experience which were not readily apparent from other sources of information, including the interviews with informed persons and with home purchasers.[1] In addition, it was hoped that the financial data would suggest new and better interpretations of the responses that home purchasers made to the questionnaires.

Where the financial data raised questions rather than answered them, the opinions of brokers and lenders were sought. These persons usually cleared up surface conflicts, but the reader will find that several issues still remain about which there may be speculation but little agreement even among persons in daily contact with the market.

There were 3,355 recorded transactions in the four study areas combined. Of these, only the financial characteristics of the bona fide, single-family home sales were studied. This resulted in the rejection of data for over 1,000 conveyances involving commercial and industrial properties or multiple dwellings, mortgage foreclosures, blanket transfers, nominal considerations and properties with wrong addresses. After the culling process, the 2,340 remaining transactions were analyzed. These constituted almost 9 percent of all bona fide home sales in the city of Philadelphia in 1955, and they included approximately 30 percent of all purchases by Negroes.[2]

The aggregate value of these sales of single-family homes in the mixed study areas was $16,500,000, and they were financed by over $13,600,000 of mortgage capital. The sales were equivalent to almost one-half of the number and one-fourth of the aggregate value of new single family homes started in the city of Philadelphia in 1955.[3]

---

[1] See Appendix C for a description of the methods employed to obtain this information and of the limitations of the data.

[2] Total bona fide single-family home sales were estimated by assuming them to be equal to about 61 percent of total deed recordings, since that percentage prevailed in the immediate past years. The estimate of total city-wide sales to Negroes is derived from unpublished data of the U. S. Bureau of the Census, *1956 National Housing Inventory.*

[3] In 1955, 5,034 single-family units were started in the city of Philadelphia. Their estimated mean sales price was $12,500, according to estimates based on unpublished data of the U. S. Department of Labor, Bureau of Labor Statistics.

THE FINANCING OF HOME PURCHASES

An understanding of any real estate market hinges to a considerable degree upon a comprehension of the role of mortgage financing. Credit makes and shapes the market.[4] In racially changing areas, mortgage lending policies play a particularly crucial role in regulating both white and nonwhite demand and thus in controlling the rate and direction of transition. The strategic importance of this market factor in the study areas is seen in the fact that 90 percent of the white buyers and 99 percent of the Negro buyers had to depend on mortgage financing to acquire their homes.

A number of discriminatory practices have been ascribed to mortgage lenders in various parts of the country. It has been asserted that lending institutions refuse to grant mortgages to Negroes on the same terms as whites, that they will not finance acquisitions in racially changing areas, and that they are reluctant to participate in a transaction which will alter the racial characteristics of a neighborhood. The purpose of this section is to explore the validity of these assertions with respect to the study areas.

Sources of mortgage funds.—Home financing in the four study areas came almost completely from established institutional sources with over 120 different institutions participating in the provision of funds. There appeared to be no difference in the types of lenders who provided mortgages for whites and nonwhites, although the latter group made somewhat greater use of savings and loan associations. Absentees depended much more heavily on individual lenders than did either group of owner occupants (table 20).[5]

Savings and loan associations furnished almost three-fourths of the financing for Negroes, 57 percent for whites, and 56 percent for absentees. Mortgage service companies provided funds for 13

---

[4] For a general examination of the financing of home ownership, see Ernest M. Fisher, *Urban Real Estate Markets: Characteristics and Financing* (New York: National Bureau of Economic Research, Inc., 1951), chap. 4.

[5] The expressions "Negro purchaser," "Negro buyer," "white purchaser," "white buyer," etc., which are used throughout this discussion, refer only to the purchasers who bought for owner-occupancy. Persons who did not occupy the houses which they purchased, viz. absentee owners, were not identified as to race.

percent of the Negro, 16 percent of the white, and only 3 percent of the absentee buyers. The corresponding figures for financing of Negro, white, and absentee acquisitions by banks and insurance companies were 10, 18, and 13 percent, respectively. The distribution of financing activity among the various types of lenders corresponded roughly with the distribution of activity among these lenders in the city as a whole.

TABLE 20

MORTGAGE TRANSACTIONS BY RACE AND TYPE OF PURCHASER, ALL STUDY AREAS, 1955

Characteristics of mortgage transaction	Owner-occupant purchasers				Absentee purchasers		Total purchasers	
	White		Negro					
	No.	Pct.	No.	Pct.	No.	Pct.	No.	Pct.
Total purchasers	443	100.0	1,574	100.0	323	100.0	2,340	100.0
Mortgage financed purchases	400	90.4	1,566	99.4	261	80.8	2,227	95.2
Type of mortgagee								
S & L associations	229	57.2	1,144	73.0	146	55.9	1,519	68.2
Mortgage service cos.	62	15.5	206	13.2	9	3.4	277	12.4
Other institution	73	18.3	150	9.6	34	13.1	257	11.5
Individuals	30	7.5	45	2.9	42	16.1	117	5.3
Miscellaneous	6	1.5	21	1.3	30	11.5	57	2.6
Total	400	100.0	1,566	100.0	261	100.0	2,227	100.0
Ratio of loan to sales price								
.90–1.00	167	41.8	1,004	64.2	57	21.8	1,228	55.1
.80–.89	72	18.0	264	16.8	55	21.1	391	17.6
Below .80	153	38.2	277	17.7	113	43.3	543	24.4
No information	8	2.0	21	1.3	36	13.8	65	2.9
Total	400	100.0	1,566	100.0	261	100.0	2,227	100.0
Interest Rate								
4½ percent or less	229[a]	57.3	1,166	74.5	55	21.1	1,450	65.1
5 to 5½ percent	73	18.3	58	3.7	36	13.8	168	7.6
6 percent and over	91	22.7	317	20.2	141	54.0	548	24.6
No information	7	1.7	25	1.6	29	11.1	61	2.7
Total	400	100.0	1,566	100.0	261	100 0	2,227	100.0

[a]Includes two mortgages carrying an interest rate of 4¾ percent.

The sources and types of mortgagees which are often associated with declining areas, or dilapidated structures, or poor mortgage risks were of negligible importance. Individuals and groups, such as lodges and clubs, together accounted for only 8 percent of the white and 3 percent of the Negro mortgages. Purchase money mortgages, almost all of which were held by individuals, totaled less than 2 percent for both whites and Negroes, and "subject" mortgages were even less numerous.[6]

The lending was heavily concentrated among a few institutions. In West Philadelphia, for example, almost 200 transactions were financed by a single company, and the eight most active lenders accounted for 52 percent of the loans. For all four study areas, most of the loans were provided by medium-sized or large institutions. Three-quarters were made by mortgagees with assets in excess of $10,000,000, whereas only 5 percent came from sources with assets of less than $1,000,000.

Only a negligible number of loans came from Negro financial sources. There are only four Negro managed savings and loan associations in Philadelphia, and their assets range from less than $300,000 to about $3,000,000. There are, in addition, two Negro-managed life insurance companies which conduct business in the city. All told, only two Negro institutions participated in the financing of homes in the study areas and extended credit to fewer than ten purchasers.

It was found in a study of racially changing areas in Chicago that mortgage funds in neighborhoods of recent transition tended to come generally from lenders located some distance from the area.[7] To see whether this was also true in the study areas, mortgagees were divided into two groups: (1) those that had offices located within ten blocks of the study areas, be they main offices or branches, and (2) those that were located elsewhere. The institutions in the latter groups were scattered throughout the city. Approximately 45 percent of both the white purchasers and Negro purchasers received their financing from nearby sources. More-

---

[6] When a mortgaged property is transferred and the purchaser assumes the responsibility for keeping up the payments on the outstanding debt, the property is said to have been transferred subject to an existing mortgage. The mortgage itself is frequently referred to as a subject mortgage. If the purchaser defaults, the lender usually still has recourse to the original borrower. Subject mortgages are frequently, but not necessarily, associated with properties or purchasers that established lending institutions regard as inferior financial risks.

It is known that there were some lease-purchase agreements, but these could not be identified from the records and informed persons were not in agreement regarding the frequency of their use. See Appendix C.

[7] E. F. Schietinger, "Racial Succession and Changing Property Values in Residential Chicago" (Ph.D. thesis, Department of Sociology, University of Chicago, 1953, dittoed), p. 172.

over, the institution that made the largest number of loans was located within one of the study areas itself. Even the first non-white purchasers on all-white blocks had no difficulty obtaining local financing.[8]

Mortgage terms.—The records indicate that Negro purchasers obtained mortgage terms that were somewhat more liberal than those advanced to whites. Among those Negro buyers who obtained mortgage loans, one-third were able to borrow 100 percent of the purchase price. An additional one-third received at least 90 percent financing. The corresponding percentages for whites were only 18 percent and 25 percent respectively, and for absentees 11 percent and 15 percent. The same picture is reflected in the structure of interest rates. The modal rate for both whites and Negroes was 4½ percent. Over one-fourth of the loans to whites, however, were at 5½ percent or better, whereas only one-fifth of the Negroes paid a rate that high. The modal rate for absentees was 6 percent. The superior terms received by Negroes are largely explained by the higher proportion of VA and FHA loans made to this group. In fact, mortgage lending throughout the study areas was characterized by an extensive use of government-insured or guaranteed loans.

As would be expected from the extensive use of FHA and VA loans, the incidence of junior financing was very low. Not only do government insured mortgages cover a high proportion of the purchase price, but regulations governing their use prohibit junior liens. Thus, the second mortgage is an accompaniment, where it occurs, of the conventional mortgage. In all, there were 38 second and no third mortgages recorded in over 2,300 transactions. The small number of junior liens which were recorded is in striking contrast to the frequent use of secondary financing by Negro home buyers in prior years.

A large majority of the FHA and VA mortgages were originated by savings and loan associations, despite the fact that conventional mortgages normally constitute at least 80 percent of the portfolios of these companies. The higher interest rates which are paid by savings and loan associations coupled with the higher operating expenses of these companies make the granting of many

---

[8] See chap. v.

government-insured loans at a fixed rate of 4½ percent disadvantageous. The willingness of the associations to make VA and FHA loans in 1955 is explained by the fact that they charged "points" to raise the effective rate of interest. Points were also charged by other lenders who made loans at 4½ percent on recent construction, but who felt that the mortgages on older properties typical of the study areas should produce a higher yield because of the shorter remaining economic life of the structures.

"Points" or "percentage points" are equivalent to a discount on FHA or VA loans and are analogous to the difference between market price and face value of bonds selling below par. They are charged when the going rate of interest on prime mortgages exceeds the fixed rate of the government-insured or guaranteed mortgages. In such a situation, a lender may not feel justified in granting VA or FHA loans unless the effective rate of interest on these loans is raised. This is done by requiring the buyer or the seller to pay the lender a sum of money which will bring the yield on the loan up to the current market interest rate. For example, if a buyer wanted a $10,000, 25-year, 4½ percent VA mortgage at a time when the safest conventional mortgages brought 5½ percent, the lender would, if he accepted the mortgage at all, require the payment of enough cash—in this case $950—to bring the effective rate of interest up to 5½ percent. An extra one or two points might be charged, i.e., the interest rate further increased, if the mortgaged property were old or in inferior condition.

This practice was most prevalent in the case of VA mortgages. Although VA regulations specifically prohibit the buyer from paying the charge, in practice the actual cash may come from the buyer, the seller, the broker, or all three, depending on market conditions and the bargaining position of the participants.[9] In Philadelphia, where the typical charge in 1955 was five points, the payment was usually made by the seller, though occasionally the

---

[9] Fortunately, the practice of paying points does not unduly complicate the interpretation of the price information in the public records. The recorded purchase price is the actual price paid by the buyer, unless the buyer makes an unrecorded cash disbursement. Such an event is said to have been rare in 1955. Similarly, the recorded interest rate is the actual interest rate on the mortgage. The recorded data are misleading in that the recorded interest rates are less than the yield to the lenders and the prices received by the sellers are less than recorded prices. These problems are secondary in most parts of the analysis.

broker contributed one or two points. Most observers felt, however, that the actual burden of the points did not fall on the seller. Liberal VA appraisals and a strong market enabled sellers to net as much as they would have if the buyer had obtained a conventional mortgage.[10] Sellers who did not have to pay points were evidently willing to accept lower prices than sellers who did have to make such payments. A few sellers, however, received windfall gains from buyers who obtained conventional mortgages, but who did not realize that prices were inflated because of liberal VA appraisals and the discounting of VA mortgages.

Mortgage discounts in some cities have been higher in mixed neighborhoods than in all-white areas and higher for persons who sell to Negroes than for those who sell to whites.[11] In West Philadelphia, however, lenders and brokers who were questioned on this matter all agreed that the discounts did not in any way reflect the racial characteristics of the area, nor did the discounts differ according to race of buyer. The practice of charging points made financing possible for many home purchasers who would otherwise not have been able to obtain loans. Lenders, despite the fairly ample supply of money during most of 1955, would not or could not make many VA and FHA 4½ percent loans. A large majority of buyers, on the other hand, could not meet the down payment requirements of conventional loans. A segment of demand would have disappeared completely but for the FHA and VA financing. The reduced prices which would have accompanied this attrition in demand would not have been sufficient to offset it, because for most buyers the down payment, not the price, was the limiting factor. Lower prices, furthermore, would undoubtedly have resulted in fewer houses being offered for sale. Thus, through the charging of points the needs of buyers, sellers, and mortgage lenders were satisfied and transactions became possible.

Have lending policies changed?—From the data presented above, it is quite evident that the study areas were financially well

---

[10] One lender reported that VA appraisals were so liberal that sellers sometimes were able to make the down payment for the buyers, as well as pay points, and still receive a net price equal to what they had originally hoped to obtain.

[11] See, for example, Chester Rapkin, Eunice Grier, and George Grier, *Group Relations in Newark, 1957, A Report to the Mayor's Commission on Group Relations* (New York: Urban Research, September, 1957), chap. v.

serviced. Mortgage funds came from a large number of established repositories of savings rather than from individuals or other unorganized sectors of the mortgage market. Negroes and whites alike were able to obtain very liberal credit terms, particularly considering the age of the properties on which loans were made. Thus, despite the recency of the transition and the racial mixture of the areas, purchasers appear to have had no unusual difficulties in obtaining the necessary financing for the acquisition of their homes.

There can be little doubt that the ready availability of liberal loans was a key factor shaping the racial transition. Moreover, this situation, while not unique, certainly has not been the rule either in Philadelphia or in other cities.[12] How then can the attitude of mortgagees toward Negro buyers in the study area be explained?

First, it should be remembered that the loans were both safe and profitable. The vast majority of the loans were insured or guaranteed. The houses on which mortgages were placed were old but in good condition. Futhermore, because of the willingness of sellers to pay "points," lenders were able to combine the extra safety of insured mortgages with the higher rate of return characteristic of conventional financing. If they decided to liquidate the loans in the secondary market, there was the knowledge that this could be done easily without risk of loss or possibly even with a small profit. Under these circumstances, liberal financing for both whites and Negroes becomes more readily understood.[13]

Second, the policies of lenders were influenced to a considerable extent by the easy money market during part of 1955, coupled with the virtual disappearance of white demand from some parts of the areas. It could be argued, of course, that the dearth of white buyers was the result, rather than the cause, of the mortgage policies toward Negroes. Although this may have been partially true, market observers felt that the decline in white demand preceded the change in the attitude of lenders. In any event, had mort-

---

[12] For a discussion of the home financing problems of nonwhites in another northern city see *ibid.*

[13] Of greater significance, therefore, may be the proportion and characteristics of Negroes who were *denied* loans, as compared with the proportion and characteristics of whites who were also denied credit. Unfortunately, no data were available on this aspect of mortgage-lending policy.

gagees not catered to Negroes in West Philadelphia and in other areas, they very likely would have been burdened with excess reserves. This was probably an especially important consideration to the large number of savings and loan associations who do not have ready outlets for their money in other areas or in other forms of investment. To survive, they were forced to accommodate to the changing scene more quickly than were the other organizations.

It appears, therefore, that although the number of Negroes who obtained loans and the liberal terms which they received cannot fail to be impressive, the 1955 experience alone does not necessarily indicate permanent change in mortgage lending policies. With a tightening of the mortgage market, there is no assurance that transitional areas will not again be shunned by many lenders repeating the experience of previous home financing cycles. During the 1920's when money was readily available, qualified Negroes met with few rebuffs in the mortgage market. In the depression of the 1930's, however, sources of credit to Negroes virtually disappeared, and nonwhite purchases were limited almost completely to foreclosed properties. This cycle was repeated in a general way in Philadelphia after World War II when several years of easy credit were followed by the tight money period of the early 1950's.

But despite past fluctuations, mortgage-lending policies have, nevertheless, been accompanied by definite signs of a trend away from discrimination. The number of institutions that will not lend to Negroes has become very small indeed, and the tendency to require higher interest rates, shorter amortization periods, and larger down payments of Negro buyers has shown a marked decline. Within this context, the data can be interpreted with much more optimism. They provide one more bit of evidence that lenders in Philadelphia are finding that there is no rational basis for applying a separate set of loan criteria to Negro mortgage applicants.

HOUSE PRICES: THEIR ROLE AND RESPONSE

Price in any market represents the resolution of a multitude of factors that enter into the shaping of supply and demand. Ordinarily, the analysis of prices is undertaken as a means of illuminating these forces and understanding their operation. In most situations the commodity that is the subject of study has little emotional content. The discussion of house prices in mixed areas, however, is highly charged.

There are a number of widely circulated theories regarding the role and reaction of house prices during a period of racial transition. The most frequent assertion that prices will slump is a major rallying point around which resistance to Negro entry is mobilized. Many a family that would otherwise have no objections to residing in a mixed area balks at the possibility of experiencing a substantial capital loss, particularly if the property is heavily encumbered with mortgage debt.[14]

Another commonly held view is that the changing neighborhood consists in reality of two housing markets, one for whites and another for Negroes. In this situation it is alleged that, in general, Negroes tend to acquire homes of low value and that they are compelled to pay more for these dwellings than whites pay for equivalent or better accommodations. This section of the report presents data from the study areas that reveal experience contrary to these widely held views.

Prices paid by Negro and white families.—The opinion that Negro purchasers in changing neighborhoods acquire the less expensive homes undoubtedly stems from the knowledge that nonwhites in general are concentrated in the lower income groups. The pattern of purchases in any specific neighborhood, however, cannot be inferred from characteristics of the population at large. In the four study areas, the average purchase price in 1955 was virtually identical for homes acquired by both Negroes and whites (table 21). For the former group it was $7,340 and for the latter $7,345. Prices ranged from under $3,000 to $18,000, but 70 percent of the houses fell between $5,000 and $9,000. Prices paid by white pur-

---

[14] The pervasiveness of this view is displayed by a recent study in Newark in which a sample of 2,126 homeowners were questioned regarding their opinions as to the effect on property values of Negro movement into white areas. Among white respondents, 2 percent felt that values would rise, 75 percent that values would decline, and 11 percent that no change would occur. The remainder did not reply. Among the Negroes interviewed, 11 percent were of the opinion that prices would rise, 33 percent felt that they would fall, 35 percent that no change would occur, and the remainder did not know or did not reply. See *Newark—A City in Transition*, prepared by Market Planning Corporation for the Newark Mayor's Commission on Group Relations, 1959.

TABLE 21

PRICE AND ASSESSED VALUE DATA BY RACE AND TYPE OF PURCHASER,
ALL STUDY AREAS, 1955

Item	Owner-occupant purchasers			Absentee purchasers	Total purchasers
	White	Negro	Total		
Number of sales	443	1,574	2,017	323	2,340
Mean sales price	$7,345	$7,340	$7,340	$5,365	$7,070
Median sales price	$7,300	$7,320	$7,315	$5,070	$7,140
Mean assessed value	$4,365	$3,890	$3,995	$3,430	$4,615
Median assessed value	$4,140	$3,800	$3,890	$3,285	$4,425
Mean sales price–assessed value ratio	1.68	1.89	1.84	1.56	1.81
Median sales price– assessed value ratio	1.75	1.92	1.88	1.58	1.86

chasers, were spread over a wider range so that a larger proportion of acquisitions by this group were to be found in the higher and in the lower brackets. Approximately 64 percent of the houses acquired by white purchasers carried a selling price between $5,000 and $9,000 with 14 percent in the group below and 22 percent in the group above that range. More than three-quarters of the houses bought by Negroes were in this middle range, with seven percent under $5,000 and the rest over $10,000. Thus, although there was some variation in the distribution of house prices, the bulk of the acquisitions by members of each race were units of moderate price.

There was considerable variation in the quality of homes purchased depending on the area in which the acquisition occurred. The highest priced units were transferred in West Philadelphia, where the average acquisition cost for Negroes and whites alike was $8,300. Home prices were considerably lower in both Strawberry Mansion and in Tasker, where the averages were $6,000 and $4,880, respectively. In Strawberry Mansion, Negroes paid considerably more on the average than did whites. The mean price for Negro purchases was $6,315 as compared with only $5,110 for white acquisitions. In Tasker the reverse was true. Whites paid $5,600 on the average as contrasted with $4,820 for Negroes. Thus, although the aggregate statistics show little price variation by race of purchasers, there is considerable difference within the sub-groups.

Bargaining effectiveness of whites and Negroes.—It is commonly held that Negroes are in such dire need of adequate housing that they are usually forced to pay premium prices for shelter. This view has given rise to the theory that there appear to be two housing markets—one for whites and another for Negroes. When a Negro acquires a dwelling in a white neighborhood, it is asserted he is usually required to pay a price higher than that which existed prior to his entry. Thus, in an area in which dwellings had formerly sold for $10,000 on the average, a Negro would pay as much as $12,000. On the other hand, should a dwelling in the same area be sold to a white purchaser, the previous price would most likely remain unchanged. One may ask: Why should an owner sell his house for a low price to a white purchaser when he could presumably obtain a much greater amount from a Negro? In this situation it is, of course, evident that in the absence of a neighborhood effort to the contrary, the owner will indeed sell to a Negro family if one can be found. If Negro housing demand is limited, then he must sell to a white if at all. A white purchaser, however, will only accept the dwelling at a substantial discount because of the existence of Negro residents in the area; but at a low price the unit is a bargain and may compensate for whatever feelings he may have regarding the existence of Negroes in the area. Thus, regardless of the general movement of prices in the mixed area, Negro buyers will tend to pay more than whites for comparable structures. This, in essence, is the theory of the dual market.

In order to shed some light on this question, two measures of relative bargaining effectiveness were devised for West Philadelphia. The first measure was based upon a comparison of prices paid by Negroes and whites for similar homes, and the second upon a comparison of ratios of sales price to assessed value for homes purchased by each of the two groups.

In the first test, situations were examined in which whites and Negroes purchased houses which were built in the same year, in the same block, on the same side of the street, and which had the same assessed values and appeared from exterior inspection to be in about the same condition. In each instance, the houses which were compared had, at the time of construction, been identical and had sold for the same price. By 1955, the houses undoubtedly varied with respect to interior condition and the amount of extras that were included in the sales price. It was assumed, however, that in the case of such closely similar houses Negroes could be expected to have purchased the superior house of the pair as often as not. Therefore, if they bargained as well as whites, they could also be expected to have paid, on the average, the same prices as whites.

There were 42 cases in which Negro and white purchases could be paired. In 23 of these cases, Negroes paid more than whites. In 17 cases, whites paid more than Negroes. In two cases, identical prices were paid. When Negroes paid more than whites, the mean excess was 9.3 percent. When whites paid more than Negroes, the mean excess was 8.6 percent. The average purchase price for whites was $7,420 and for Negroes $7,625. Thus, although the whites did slightly better, the differences were not important. Furthermore, some of the variation appears to have been due to the more liberal financing received by Negroes.

The second test compared the aggregate ratio of sales price to assessed value (SP–AV) for white purchases with the corresponding aggregate ratio for Negro purchases in West Philadelphia as a whole. If it can be assumed that appraisals for tax purposes, virtually all of which were made prior to extensive Negro occupancy, do not differ on the average for houses purchased by Negroes and by whites, then differences in the ratio of selling price to assessed value constitute a measure of price comparison.[15] It was found that the Negro ratio was 1.85 and the white ratio only 1.65 suggesting that whites obtained considerably more for their housing dollar than did Negroes. When the ratios were standardized for location of purchase and lending terms, however, the difference between them disappeared for some groups of buyers (see Appendix D, table D-21). However, Negroes who obtained loan-value ratios of less than 0.90 had higher SP–AV ratios and thus perhaps bargained less effectively than did the corresponding group of white purchasers. Nevertheless, according to the second

---

[15] For a discussion of the SP–AV ratio see Appendix C.

measure a majority of Negroes and whites appeared to have received about the same value for their housing dollar.

Although the above findings show that Negro buyers did almost as well as white purchasers at the level of the financial transaction, it cannot be inferred that equality extended to all matters which affected the prices paid by the two groups. It was reported that attempts were made to prevent Negroes from acquiring homes in portions of Zones 4 and 5 where prices appear to have been the most attractive. In addition, it is known that many Negroes in West Philadelphia and in the rest of the city were victims of unconscionable charges at settlements.[16] It is evident, therefore, that full equality for Negroes in the Philadelphia housing market still awaits the elimination of residual forms of price discrimination.

Price trends in mixed neighborhoods.—Numerous theories have been advanced regarding the behavior of house prices in neighborhoods entered by Negroes. The earliest view held that Negro entry almost invariably results in price declines.[17] Although this belief still has wide acceptance among the public at large, it has given way to more sophisticated views in the professional literature.

Schietinger, for example, has related price movements to stages of Negro entry, holding that the mere "threat" of such an event may cause a dip in prices, but that when nonwhite purchases finally take place, prices usually recover.[18] Several writers have suggested that price declines in transitional areas have a greater probability of occurring among homes in the more expensive brackets.[19] Still other analysts have stressed the influence of panic selling, the state of the market, the social structure of the community,

---

[16] Evidence of unconscionable charges were found in the files of the Philadelphia Jewish Community Relations Council, Committee on Fair Housing Practices.

[17] Some of the earlier views are reviewed in Charles Abrams, *Forbidden Neighbors* (New York: Harper and Brothers, 1955).

[18] Schietinger, "Racial Succession and Changing Property Values. . . ," p. 210.

[19] See Belden Morgan, "Values in Transition Areas: Some New Concepts," *The Review of the Society of Residential Appraisers*, XVIII, no. 3 (March, 1952), 5-10. See also, George A. Phillips, "Racial Infiltration," *The Review of the Society of Residential Appraisers*, XVI, no. 2 (February, 1950), 8. For an opposite point of view, see Thurston H. Ross, "Market Significance of Declining Neighborhoods," *The Appraisal Journal*, XXIII, no. 2 (April, 1955), 203-211.

and the personalities of individuals affected by Negro entry. It
has also been pointed out that perhaps the principal reason why
an owner may think Negro in-migration causes prices to dip is
that when such entry occurs the neighborhood may lose its value
to him and he thinks only in terms of selling to another person
like himself.[20]

In order to investigate the impact of transition on home values,
a price index was constructed for West Philadelphia, the only
area where sufficient observations were available for this purpose.
Ordinarily the construction of a house price index would be a research project in itself. The heterogeneity of the housing stock,
the spottiness of sales, and the changing universe over time raise
complicated problems of index construction and sample design.
Furthermore, the data-gathering process is expensive and time con-
suming because of the difficulties involved in separating bona fide
single-family home transfers from all other types of market conveyances.

It was feasible to construct a price index for this study only by
circumventing, if not meeting, these formidable obstacles. In tran-
scribing the 1955 sales data, the previous price and date of each
property transferred was also recorded. This made possible a price
index based on a variation of the Wyngarten method.[21] Although
this approach does not overcome all of the problems of price
index construction, it yields a generally satisfactory measure of
price changes. The method consists essentially of selecting properties which have been sold more than once during the period
covered by the index, calculating price relatives for these properties, and combining the price relatives into an index. Using this
technique, a price relative for each year from 1947 through 1955
was calculated by dividing the total acquisition cost of houses
acquired in a given year by their aggregate sales price in 1955.
These relatives were then converted to a 1949 base.

---

[20] Herbert J. Gans, "Status and Residential Property Value" (Institute for Urban
Studies, University of Pennsylvania, June, 1954), p. 13 (unpublished).

[21] Herman Wyngarten, "An Index of Local Real Estate Prices," *Michigan Business Studies,* University of Michigan, January, 1927. For a more complete ex-
planation of the method, see David M. Blank, "Relationship Between an Index
of House Prices and Building Costs," *Journal of the American Statistical Association,* vol. 49 (1954), 67-68.

The price index thus derived shows a gradual upward movement from 100 in 1949 to 107 in 1953. This trend is reversed by a sharp drop to 98 in 1954 which, in turn, is followed by an equally sharp recovery in 1955 to a high of 117 (figure 11, solid line).

The sharp drop of the index in 1954 is due to a limitation of the Wyngarten method. The technique does not account for possible differences between long- and short-term holdings. It ignores, therefore, the question of whether the individual who bought a home in West Philadelphia in 1948, or one of the earlier years, and who sold in 1955 purchased the same type of house as did the person who acquired a dwelling in 1954 only to sell it the following year.[22]

When this question was investigated, it was discovered that 55 percent of the homes which were bought in 1954 and sold in 1955 had been sold in the later year by absentees. In contrast, the proportion of 1955 absentee sellers involved in sales of homes acquired in earlier years was only about 10 percent. It was further noted that the gross profit realized by the 1955 absentee sellers who had held their properties for only one or two years was in excess of 20 percent, or more than double the gross realized by the corresponding group of owner-occupant sellers. For these reasons, the 1954 price relative seemed especially unrepresentative and was, therefore, adjusted by rejecting on a random basis nine out of every ten of the transactions involving absentees. This procedure made the proportion of absentees for all years roughly the same and minimized the influence of the short-term investment

---

[22] The principal limitation of the index, other than that mentioned, relates to the 1955 sales which form the basic sample. They were not randomly selected, but instead include all properties which were sold. As a result, the structures in the mixed zones where the rate of turnover was in excess of 9 percent receive weights which are disproportionately high with respect to homes in the white section where the turnover rate was less than 5 percent. In addition, the homes which comprise the sample change annually, and in any single year could be unrepresentative, not only of the universe of houses, but also of the universe of sales. This possibility is particularly to be noted because the average annual sample of 56 sales is less than 6 percent of the "normal" turnover in the study area. The problem of annual variations in the sample did not appear to be severe because the sales which comprised the index showed a fairly constant distribution from year to year, both among the five zones and among the three classes of 1955 purchasers. Thus, although the sales may have been unrepresentative of the total universe of houses, their annual bias was consistent with respect to the variables mentioned.

activity reflected in the original 1954 relative. The adjustment raised the 1954 index from 98 to 104.

Price movements by subsection.—It is quite apparent that transition in West Philadelphia was accompanied by a substan-

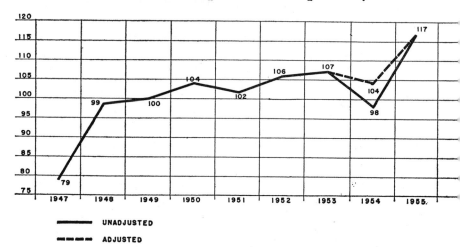

Fig. 11. Single-family house-price index, West Philadelphia study area, 1947–1955.

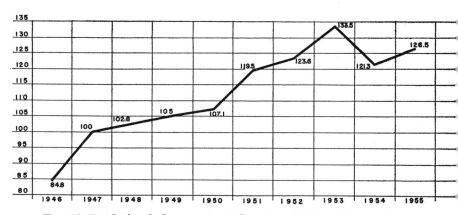

Fig. 12. Single-family house-price index, city of Philadelphia, 1946–1955.

tial price advance. The price movements do not appear, however, to have departed radically from those for the entire city. Two price indexes for the city show a rise from 1950 to 1953 of roughly the same magnitude (figures 12 and 13). In addition, the city index

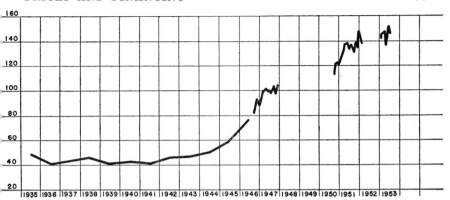

SOURCE: DATA FROM HOUSING AND HOME FINANCE AGENCY.

Fig. 13. Index of asking prices of existing (other than new) single-family houses, Philadelphia, 1935–1953—April–June, 1947=100.

which continues beyond 1953 reflects the same leveling off of prices which was observed in the study area.

It cannot be concluded from the similarity of the West Philadelphia and city-wide trends that Negro entry had no price effect. Two other explanations seem more tenable: (1) in the absence of Negro entry, the West Philadelphia market would have suffered a decline, or (2) the volume of Negro demand was just about equal to the attrition in white demand which was caused by Negro entry. To examine these possible explanations, a comparison was made of the experience in the areas entered by Negroes with that in the sections where little or no nonwhite in-migration had taken place.

Two additional price indexes were constructed for separate parts of the study area—the first for Zones 1 and 2, and a second index for Zones 3, 4, and 5. This division had the additional effect of partially compensating for the uneven area distribution of the sales. Some unevenness remained, nevertheless, because Zone 3 with a rate of turnover of more than 7 percent in 1955 accounted for slightly more than half of the sales in the yearly samples for Zones 3, 4, and 5 combined. Zone 3 was included with the white zones instead of with the mixed zones because, until 1955, Negroes comprised considerably less than 5 percent of the Zone 3 population and, therefore, could not have had any direct impact on most of the area prior to that time.

The differential price behavior in the two sections selected for comparison is significant. In Zones 1 and 2—the sections of heavy Negro entry—there was a steady price climb from 1948 to 1955 with only a temporary cessation from 1952 to 1954 (figure 14). The index supports the view of brokers that there was a slight dip from 1952 through early 1955. In contrast, it may be noted that in Zones 3, 4, and 5 there was a mild price decline which started in 1949 and which, except for a temporary recovery during the boom construction year of 1950, continued unabated through 1952. Prices then began to recover and continued upward through 1955[23] (figure 15). It would be unwise to place too much emphasis on the detailed movements of the two series because the samples on which they are based are relatively small. Nevertheless, the over-all divergence does not appear to be a chance occurrence and even if the fluctuations are interpreted only in their broadest context, three significant facts emerge.

First, and most important, is that a price decline evidently began in the white section prior to any reasonable expectation of nonwhite occupancy in the area. It would seem that most of

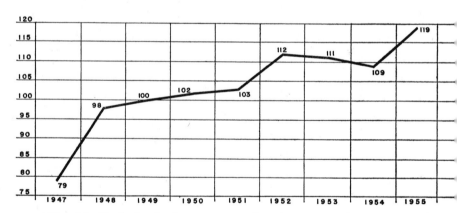

Fig. 14. Single-family house-price index, Zones 1 and 2, West Philadelphia study area, 1947–1955.

---

[23] In comparing figures 14 and 15, the reader must bear in mind that the magnitudes measure percentage differences from 1949. Thus, the 1956 relative of 119 in figure 14 when compared with the corresponding relative of 112 in figure 15 does not mean that prices in 1956 were necessarily higher in Zones 1 and 2 than in Zones 3, 4, and 5, but only that they had risen more since 1949.

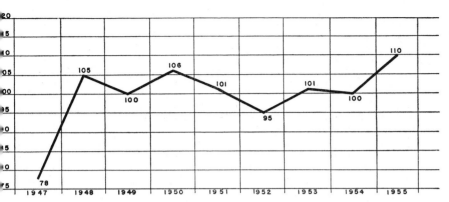

Fig. 15. Single-family house-price index, Zones 3, 4, and 5, West Philadelphia study area, 1947–1955.

the downward shift in prices in these zones was due to factors other than the threat of Negro entry. Thus, the data lend some support to the "soft spot" theory which holds that the threat of Negro entry is seldom the cause of price declines; rather that Negroes tend to enter areas in which white demand has already been on the wane for other reasons and in which, therefore, sales began to weaken and prices have slackened.

Second, the apparent recovery of the market from 1953 to 1955 took place during a period in which Negro entry became imminent in some parts of the area and an accomplished fact in others. The recovery is even more notable since it coincides with a general easing of the housing shortage throughout the city. The upturn may have been partially due to Negro entry in Zone 3, but it must be kept in mind that the recovery began before nonwhite purchases in Zone 3 had reached a sizable proportion of total market activity.[24]

Finally, the upward movement of prices in Zones 1 and 2 occurred in conjunction with a fairly high rate of white out-migration. The 1955 turnover rate in Zone 2, for example, exceeded 15 percent in contrast with a city-wide rate of less than 6 percent.

---

[24] Another possible interpretation of figure 15 is that prices were generally stable or declining from 1948 through 1954 and did not start their recovery until 1955 when Negro purchasers became quite numerous in Zone 3.

These data indicate that the rapid departure of white families from racially changing areas need not be associated with depressed prices.

A general statement concerning studies of price trends in mixed areas.—The popular conviction that nonwhite entry into an all-white residential area causes home prices to decline is regarded by many analysts as a major barrier to the goal of better housing for minority groups. It has been the view of these analysts that Negroes, in attempting to improve their housing situation by moving into neighborhoods occupied by white families, would meet with much less resistance were it not for the fear of home-owners that prices would surely fall. To combat this damaging and, presumably, erroneous conception, several major research efforts have been devoted to the investigation of the behavior of home prices in racially mixed areas. There is now a fair body of evidence indicating that prices often rise during, and perhaps because of, racial transition. Whether these findings will prove to be as useful as originally anticipated, however, may be questioned on several grounds.

First, it is small comfort to an institutional lender protecting other people's money, or to an owner intent on safeguarding his investment, to know that prices sometimes rise and sometimes fall when Negroes enter a neighborhood, particularly since the question seldom arises on the occasion of a white purchase. Unless predictions can be made in specific situations, the attitudes and practices of mortgagees, appraisers, brokers, and owners will not change materially, for these groups cannot be expected to take the very real risk of a possible decline. Lenders in particular are prone to take a cautious view of neighborhoods experiencing racial change until the likely long-term trend can be determined.

Second, almost without exception, Negro in-migration in the areas in which price studies have been made appeared to be associated with a visible reduction in white demand and, in many situations, an increase in the supply of houses for sale. The price reaction, therefore, was largely dependent on the extent to which Negro demand filled this partial vacuum. Prices could rise above the general level in comparable all-white neighborhoods only if Negroes had both the buying power (liquid assets and credit) to absorb all the market supply of the areas at a higher price level and the willingness to pay premiums to purchase the houses offered for sale. But Negroes could be expected to pay premium prices only if they were experiencing a housing shortage as a result of having limited access to the market. Thus, the very argument (that prices actually rise when Negroes purchase into a neighborhood) used to reduce discrimination against nonwhite home buyers is valid only when precisely the same form of discrimination exists on a wide scale.[25] It is doubtful whether potential Negro home buyers view the phenomenon of a price rise with any degree of pleasure since its cause reflects the persistence of an unhappy circumstance.

An examination of the price studies reveals yet another curious twist. In the face of an attrition of white demand, prices in a mixed neighborhood can be maintained only if Negroes continue to buy into the neighborhood and at the original price level. Thus, at the present time white residents have the choice of declining prices or an increasing number of Negro neighbors, or both. There are few instances of firm or rising prices and a stable mixed neighborhood being achieved simultaneously.[26] In view of these facts, it could be argued that the effect of the price studies might be to solidify resistance to Negro entry or at best to assist white residents in deciding the most propitious time to sell.

In their zeal to show that Negro entry has a beneficial effect on the market, analysts have tended to overlook these aspects of rising prices. They have also glossed over the reasons for price declines. For example, one author states "It is the mass exodus that temporarily gluts the market with offerings that depresses prices,

---

[25] Or when most white buyers cease to avoid mixed areas. The argument—in milder form—that prices do not fall when Negroes enter a neighborhood would also be valid in the rare situation when the reduction in white demand is exactly offset by the increase in Negro demand and market supply does not increase or decrease.

[26] Principally in situations of isolated Negro entry, see Luigi Laurenti, *Property Values and Race: Studies in Seven Cities* (Berkeley: University of California Press, 1960), chaps. vi, vii, and xi. See also Arnold M. Rose, Frank P. Atelsek, and Lawrence R. McDonald, "Neighborhood Reactions to Isolated Negro Residents: An Alternative to Invasion and Succession," *American Sociological Review*, vol. 18, no. 5 (October, 1953), 497-507. Also Henry G. Stetler, *Racial Integration in Private Residential Neighborhoods in Connecticut* (Hartford: State of Connecticut Commission on Civil Rights, 1957), pp. 6-7.

not the influx. It is like a bank run engendered by fear. The fears produce an unwarranted condition that could be avoided if people would stay put."[27] Laurenti takes a similar point of view and expresses the thought that downward price movements may be largely a matter of the self-fulfilling prophecy.[28] Residents who think prices will decline try to sell their homes before the market weakens and thereby bring about the decline which they fear.

The limited applicability of these observations is readily apparent, both theoretically and in the market place itself. In sections of West Philadelphia and Strawberry Mansion white sales were substantial, yet there was sufficient Negro demand to sustain prices. In West Mount Airy, on the other hand, where the houses were expensive and nonwhite demand limited, a moderate price decline was observed in the face of no increase in the rate of white out-migration. If price declines occur in connection with a prophecy, it is more probably the unfulfilled prophecy. Many white families try to leave a mixed area in the expectation that it will soon become all Negro, rather than in anticipation of a dip in prices. If their prediction is incorrect, however, and the expected rush of Negro buyers does not materialize, prices may indeed move to a lower level.

In summary, it appears that the studies of price movements in racially mixed areas have fallen short of their basic objectives because they have focused on the price shifts themselves rather than on the full array of underlying causes of these shifts. In essence they have failed to provide any real foundation for a change in attitudes or practices toward Negroes by brokers, appraisers, mortgage lenders, and homeowners. If discrimination was good business prior to these inquiries, it is equally good business today. It is unfortunate, too, that this type of analysis carries with it the implication that the justification for a social objective such as equality of access to the housing supply must be evaluated primarily in terms of the criteria of the market place. In all fairness, however, it must be stated that the principal and permanent value of these studies may be in erasing the primitive folk notion that

---

[27] Morgan, *The Review of the Society of Residential Appraisers*, XVIII, no. 3 (March, 1952).
[28] Laurenti, *Property Values and Race.* . . , chap. ii.

Negroes have an inherent taint which inevitably causes house prices to decline in any area that they may enter. If this belief has fewer adherents as a result of these studies, then an important contribution has been made to the improvement of race relations and to the ultimate goal of equality for Negroes.

VII

The Role of the Absentee Owner

It is a common belief that areas in transition are the scene of much real estate speculation by absentee owners immediately subsequent to the first Negro entry and also during the ensuing process of racial change. Whether the experience of a particular area tends to substantiate the theory is often difficult to establish. There are intrinsic conceptual difficulties in testing this view, first because the distinction between a speculator and an investor is, within limits, a subjective determination, and second because the dividing line between much speculation and little speculation also cannot be ascertained objectively. Even so, a study of transition would not be complete without some examination of this subject.

Absentee owners quite obviously do not acquire dwellings for their own occupancy but rather for resale or rental. Every residential area of some age is characterized by a certain degree of ownership by persons who do not live on the premises. Even in recent subdivisions, families are frequently compelled to move before their homes can be sold and they may offer their units for rent in order to derive some revenue prior to disposition. In older areas volitional investment by absentee owners is observed quite commonly. In fact, transition from owner to rental occupancy is typically a part of the process of neighborhood aging. A later stage of obsolescence is often accompanied by a conversion of the larger single-family unit to smaller rental accommodations.

In areas of racial transition the absentee owner is reputed to play a special role. Because he frequently resides outside of the immediate area of transition, he has little stake in the neighborhood in which change is taking place. In many instances, the absentee owner will capitalize on the change by purchasing units at low prices from families eager to flee, in the hope that he can sell them at higher prices within a short time to members of the incoming group. It is alleged that the absentee owner is frequently one of the stimulators of panic. Observing the opportunity for rapid and substantial gain, he may attempt to hasten the transition process and therefore create a situation in which the volume of sales and his profits are appreciably increased.

The data on absentees were developed by first noting the single family home transfers in 1955 that involved an absentee buyer or seller. Tabulations were then made of the number and location of properties bought or sold by absentee owners, gross profits on sales by absentees, and the number of years that their properties had been held prior to the 1955 sales. From the resultant figures, presented in this chapter, a rough evaluation was made of the extent to which transition was accompanied and, perhaps, assisted by absentee activity and short term investment motivations.

A GENERAL PICTURE OF THE ABSENTEE MARKET

There was an appreciable amount of activity by absentee owners in the study areas in 1955 with about 14 percent of the purchases and 20 percent of the sales having been made by this group (table 22). This volume of activity does not seem excessive for Philadelphia, however, since approximately 15 percent of all occupied single-family units in the city are rented.[1]

The level of absentee participation varied among the study areas. In West Philadelphia, absentees accounted for 10 percent of the total purchases and 16 percent of the sales whereas in the Tasker area of South Philadelphia, almost one-fourth of the 1955 purchases and 37 percent of the sales were by absentees.

---

[1] This figure was taken from unpublished data of the U. S. Bureau of the Census, 1956 *National Housing Inventory*. It is true, of course, that the rented units may ordinarily turn over much *less* frequently than do the owner-occupied dwellings.

TABLE 22

OCCUPANCY STATUS OF PREVIOUS OWNERS OF SINGLE-FAMILY HOMES
PURCHASED IN 1955 BY RACE AND TYPE OF PRESENT OWNER,
ALL STUDY AREAS, 1955

Race and type of present owner	Occupancy status of previous owners					
	Owner-occupant		Absentee		Total	
	Number	Percent	Number	Percent	Number	Percent
Owner-occupant						
White	359	81.0	84	19.0	443	100.0
Negro	1,301	82.7	273	17.3	1,574	100.0
Absentee	221	68.4	102	31.6	323	100.0
Total	1,881	80.4	459	19.6	2,340	100.0

Little of the absentee activity appeared to be associated with homes which were normally in the investment market. Only 102 were made by one absentee to another; 359 of the 2,340 sales were made by absentees to owner-occupants and 221 were by owner-occupants to absentees. In all, absentees were involved in one out of every four transactions in the study areas.

With the exception of the Veterans Administration and a few financial institutions that obtained title to several dwellings through foreclosure proceedings, virtually all of the absentee buyers were private individuals, approximately half of whom lived in or near the study areas. Several of the absentee buyers were identified as persons who had not yet moved into their homes or who had moved in and out again within the space of a few months. Similarly, a small number of absentee sellers are known to have been owner-occupants until shortly before they placed their homes for sale. The vast majority of absentee buyers and sellers, however, apparently never intended to occupy their houses, but rather acquired them for investment or speculation. Sixty-five of these individuals participated in more than one transaction, and two operators—both of them real estate brokers —each bought or sold more than twenty properties each.

Absentee activity was most pronounced in the vanguard of the Negro movement and in the sections experiencing rapid Negro in-migration. In West Philadelphia, for example, buying was focused at the point of Negro entry, principally Zone 3 (table 23). It may be that the professional investors tend to buy proper-

TABLE 23

NUMBER AND PROPORTION OF TRANSACTIONS INVOLVING ABSENTEES,
ZONES 1 THROUGH 5, WEST PHILADELPHIA, 1955

Zone	Absentee buyers to total buyers		Absentee sellers to total sellers		Transactions involving absentees	
	Number	Percent	Number	Percent	Number	Percent
1	27	11.7	49	21.3	64	27.8
2	37	5.9	91	14.4	118	18.7
3	39	19.6	30	15.1	65	32.7
4	12	13.8	18	20.7	26	29.9
5	17	13.2	19	14.7	34	26.4
Total	132	10.3	207	16.2	307	24.1

ties in the path of Negro migration, sell to nonwhites, and then move on.

ABSENTEE PURCHASES

Absentee buyers paid lower prices for their properties than did persons who acquired homes for occupancy. The average payment by absentees was only $5,365 as compared with $7,340 by the latter group. The mean assessed value of houses acquired by absentees, however, was only slightly less than that for houses bought by owner-occupants, $3,430 compared with $3,995, indicating that only a small part of the difference in the average prices paid by the two groups can be attributed to basic quality differences in the houses purchased.

The lower prices paid by absentees may have been related either to the physical condition of the houses or to the bargaining position of the sellers. An inspection of the properties acquired by the various classes of buyers was not made, nor were the sellers studied, but from the SP–AV ratios it would appear that a higher proportion of absentees than owner-occupants acquired deteriorated dwellings or purchased from extremely necessitous owners or both. SP–AV ratios of less than 1.00 were encountered in 8 percent of the absentee purchases as compared with less than 1 percent for both white and Negro acquisitions. In addition, absentees also had a much higher proportion of SP–AV ratios in the 1.00 to 1.49 range.

Another factor explaining the lower prices paid by absentees may be the less liberal lending terms which they received. In order to examine this possibility the ratios of sales price to assessed value for the two categories of buyers were standardized for differences in down payments. Absentees who succeeded in securing mortgages that were between 90 and 100 percent of price paid as high a multiple of assessed value for their properties as did both Negro and white owner-occupants. Unlike both these groups, however, only a small proportion (one-sixth) of the absentees obtained high ratio loans. In fact, almost 20 percent of the absentee buyers, as compared with only 10 percent of the white buyers and less than 1 percent of the Negro buyers, did not resort to debt financing at all.

Absentees also were charged higher interest rates more often than were owner-occupants. Only one-third paid as little as 4½ percent and over one-third paid 6 percent. Although no statistical data are available on amortization periods, the higher interest rates plus the known short-term holdings of absentees indicate that many of the mortgages to absentees were in the nature of short-term commercial loans. Since conventional loans rather than FHA or VA mortgages were used, the payment of "points" which ordinarily would have been translated into higher prices was not part of the transactions.

ABSENTEE SALES

It was observed earlier that nonresident owners may expedite the process of racial transition in residential neighborhoods because they lack the type of community identification which would induce strong resistance to selling to Negroes. The West Philadelphia data lend some support to this view. Although the proportions of total purchases by whites and Negroes from absentees differed very little, 17 and 15 percent respectively, fully 33 percent of the first Negro families on the block bought from absentees.[2]

It will be remembered, however, that a sizable portion of the so-called "nonresident" sellers actually lived in or near the study areas and presumably, therefore, had at least as much community identification as did the owner-occupants. It would seem more

[2] See chap. v.

TABLE 24

NUMBER AND PROPORTION OF HOUSES SOLD IN 1955 THAT WERE OWNED LESS THAN TWO YEARS, BY TYPE OF SELLER, ZONES 1 THROUGH 5, WEST PHILADELPHIA STUDY AREA, 1955

Zone	Owner-occupant			Absentee			Total		
	Houses sold	Houses held less than two years		Houses sold	Houses held less than two years		Houses sold	Houses held less than two years	
		Number	Percent		Number	Percent		Number	Percent
1	181	16	8.9	49	24	49.0	230	40	17.3
2	540	69	12.8	91	52	57.1	631	121	19.2
3	169	15	8.8	30	19	63.3	199	34	17.1
4	69	9	13.1	18	10	55.6	87	19	21.8
5	110	11	10.0	19	10	52.6	129	21	16.3
Total	1,069	120	11.2	207	115	55.6	1,276[a]	235	18.4

[a]No information available for six sellers.

likely that transition would be facilitated principally by professional traders and to a lesser extent by the absentee owners living in other communities. When this possibility was checked for West Philadelphia, it was found that three-fourths of the absentee sales to first Negro entrants were, indeed, by individuals who were identified by local real estate brokers as market professionals and that the remaining absentee sales to the Negro "first" families were by persons who did not live in or near the study area. Moreover, only 15 percent of the transfers by the professional group were to white families, whereas the corresponding figure for sales by all absentees was nearly 30 percent.

Of the houses sold by absentees, 55 percent had been held for less than two years (table 24). By comparison, the median period of ownership for all homes sold in West Philadelphia in 1955 was about seven years.[3] There is evidence that the short-term absentee investments were indeed profitable. The mean gross profit realized by absentees on sales of properties held less than two years was 25 percent,[4] as compared with only 8 percent for sales by owner-occupants who had held their homes a similar period of time. Average gross profit on capital invested was calculated to be approximately 125 percent. Gross profits on sales to Negroes were double those obtained from sales to whites. Yet, within each zone, the median SP–AV ratios of the whites and Negroes who purchased from absentees were almost identical. This would appear to indicate that absentees tended to purchase houses below the prevalent level and that the outgoing sellers rather than the incoming Negro families provided the source of capital gain for the absentee traders. This in itself may reflect an eagerness on the part of previous owners to sell, but we do not know whether this was due to inner compulsion or to outside pressures generated by the absentee purchasers.

The known professional traders who accounted for about one-half of the short-term holdings by absentees did even better than

---

[3] Since the annual turnover rate for the city as a whole was only 6 to 7 percent, the velocity of sale in this study area was approximately twice as great as for the city as a whole. The rate of sale indicates that brokers were able to double their earnings from commissions during the period of transition.

[4] Excluding properties sold by the Veterans Administration.

the nonresident group as a whole.[5] They grossed an average of 35 percent on their quick resales. Their transactions with Negroes yielded them a gross of 40 percent and the transfers to first Negro entrants 50 percent.

Unfortunately, there is no way of determining whether net profits were as large as the gross figures would suggest. Costs of receiving and conveying title, property insurance, financing charges, and repair and rehabilitation expenditures may have absorbed much of the profit unless the houses were rented during the period of ownership. Furthermore, even assuming net incomes were quite large, there is no evidence to show that similar types of operations in white neighborhoods were any less remunerative.

CONCLUSIONS

Racial transition was accompanied by only a moderate number of real estate transactions involving short-term investors and speculators. Although market professionals no doubt did expedite the process of change, it appears that owner-occupants were instrumental in effecting the vast majority of shifts from white to nonwhite residence.

The amount of absentee activity is more notable because, while it was not exceptionally large, neither was it especially small. Although market experts evidently did not find the area unusually inviting, they were not fearful that the effect of Negro entry on house prices would preclude profitable transactions. This may be the most effective evidence to refute the notion that Negro entry always lowers prices.

---

[5] Of the properties purchased and sold by the known professionals, only one had been held more than two years.

VIII

The Prospect for Stable
Interracial Neighborhoods

The past decade has witnessed the racial transition of many neighborhoods in the city. This process has been stimulated by a rapid increase in the numbers and income of the nonwhite population, buttressed by a virtual absence of newly constructed houses available to Negroes anywhere in the metropolitan area. The most logical areas to undergo racial change, prejudices considered, were on the periphery of established nonwhite sections where a point of contact had been established, and change, since it was expected, was usually not strongly resisted. Thus, in the study areas transition was the natural extension of existing Negro neighborhoods.

The expansion of these mixed communities has, however, not been without pattern. For transition to begin in a new block or neighborhood, a portion of the supply must be made available to Negroes by white homeowners, and this usually requires a soul-searching decision. In the study areas, sales that opened blocks or neighborhoods were frequently made by professional traders and other absentee owners who presumably were subject to less community pressure than were owner-occupants. Generally speaking, however, the initial sales were made by ordinary home-owners who did not explore the possibility of selling to Negroes until it became evident that white buyers willing to pay a satisfactory price could not be found.

The contraction of white purchases was related to some extent to the proximity of Negroes themselves. As the border of the Negro community moved closer and closer to a given street front, white buyers were harder to find. Owners who had to move from the area may have preferred to sell to white families, but were unable to do so. The threat of Negro entry was, however, not the only deterrent to white acquisitions. After the postwar housing shortage had eased and new housing became readily available in the suburbs, the study areas with their old and obsolescent homes were no longer attractive to a substantial sector of the white market. Initially, in fact, the age and quality of the houses may have been the most important factor limiting white demand and, thus, promoting Negro entry.

Negro entry into white blocks was also encouraged by the absence of violence directed toward nonwhite purchasers, a response that has accompanied Negro residential expansion in most sections of the city. The vigorous action of the Philadelphia Commission on Human Relations which has stopped many potential disturbances in their nascent stages may have been a principal deterrent to violence in some areas, but it is also true that exceedingly few Negroes entered neighborhoods in which the danger signs were clear. In the study areas, there were few reported instances of hostile action toward first Negro entrants who, by and large, reported a reasonably friendly attitude on the part of white residents. This is not to suggest that there was no opposition to Negro entry, but that there were very few ugly incidents.

THE MIXED AREA HOUSING MARKET

The housing market in the study areas did not differ materially from the markets in other sections of the city. The white families who purchased homes were very much like other homeowners in the areas and similar to home purchasers in the rest of Philadelphia. The large majority were couples with children. They earned moderate incomes and engaged in a wide variety of occupations. These purchasers were not motivated by a drive to symbolize racial democracy and, in fact, many of them were not pleased by the presence of Negroes in their neighborhood.

As far as the structure of prices and home financing is concerned, Negroes and whites paid approximately the same prices for comparable houses; the usual institutional sources of mortgage funds were available to finance the purchases; and mortgage terms were extremely liberal by any standard. Equally important, the entry of Negroes was not accompanied by price declines; on the contrary, there were substantial increases in home values.

It is not unfair to say that families were attracted to the areas for commonplace reasons. First and foremost, the families sought a home in the lower price and quality levels, and although such dwellings were available in other sections of the city, the choice was somewhat limited. Their selection, however, was not made on the basis of house price alone, but was influenced also by specific advantages of the areas, such as nearness or ready access to place of employment, good transportation service, and proximity to a variety of shopping facilities. In addition, many of the purchasers were attracted by existing concentrations of persons of similar religion or national heritage. In view of these positive factors the white buyers evidently felt that the presence of Negroes was an insufficient reason to avoid the areas.

We have found that the nature of neighborhood change is by no means one-directional. The widely held view that no white will ever purchase in an area once it is entered by a Negro is in need of serious reconsideration. This is an important conclusion, but it would indeed be premature to use it as the basis for a firm generalization regarding the future of housing demand in mixed areas. Although almost five hundred white families bought homes in the mixed areas, they comprised only one-fourth of the total purchasers. Moreover, white purchases declined as the relative proportion of resident Negro population increased, and few were to be found even in sections in which the proportion of nonwhites was low. But perhaps the most important reservation of all is the fact that the number of white purchasers was not sufficient to keep the population in these areas from becoming increasingly nonwhite.

PATTERNS OF TRANSITION

The rate of racial change varied widely from neighborhood to neighborhood and even from block to block. On several street fronts, each containing as many as fifty to sixty homes, virtually the entire inventory changed from white to Negro ownership in less than three years. In other blocks, transition was much slower, with a fair proportion of white families remaining in residence five or more years after Negro entry. In the relatively expensive West Mount Airy section of Germantown, and in the low-price Tasker area of South Philadelphia, racial change with one or two short-lived exceptions proceeded at an extremely moderate rate, whereas transition in most of the Strawberry Mansion and West Philadelphia areas was quite rapid.

The variations in the rate of transition are not, as commonly thought, simply a measure of differences in the intensity and extent of prejudice and discrimination. Rather differences in rates are due to variations in all the factors analyzed in the previous chapters which affect the level of white demand, the level of Negro demand, the number and race of families who wish to sell their homes, and the interaction of these three variables. Indeed, the factors which control these variables not only fix the rate of transition, but also determine whether it will occur at all.

Rapid transition in the study areas was the product of numerous influences: liberal mortgage terms, sustained Negro demand, a substantial supply of old houses of fair quality and moderate value, rising prices, considerable activity by professional real estate operators, and ready availability of high-quality housing for whites in other sections of the city and in the suburbs. Although these factors tend to explain the fairly rapid change in two of the study areas, they do not explain the pockets of slow transition in some sections within these areas. These sections contain a larger proportion of rental units, a greater amount of land in commercial use, higher-priced homes, and parochial schools where the percentage of nonwhite students was relatively low at the time of the study.

Rapid transition in other neighborhoods in the city appeared to stem from factors identical or similar to those in West Philadelphia and Strawberry Mansion. By comparison, slow transition in other neighborhoods was associated with a moderately large percentage of low quality housing for which financing was difficult to obtain, or of expensive homes which most Negro families could not afford. Prices in these areas either were stable or rose at a slower pace than in the areas of rapid transition. White demand dropped as sharply in the neighborhoods of slow change as in the sections where the racial transformation was more rapid. In the neighborhoods of both slow and rapid change, absentee sellers, most of whom were in the market for the short run, appeared to have facilitated the transition process.

There are a number of additional factors which appeared to be vital in determining the rate of transition, even though data were lacking to demonstrate their importance. Foremost among these were expectations. The predictions of white families concerning the eventual racial mix of a neighborhood and their apprehensions regarding the possibility of inundation may be more significant than any other factor in determining the level of white demand. Yet it is largely the level of white demand that determines the eventual racial mix. Also of consequence are the demographic characteristics of the resident and in-migrant populations, the racial composition of the schools, activities of community organizations, the policies and practices of market intermediaries, and the spatial distribution of the Negro residences in the mixed area. Depending on the interaction of these and the other variables discussed above, transition may be fast or slow or may not occur at all; there may be transition without discrimination or discrimination without transition.

THE FUTURE OF RESIDENTIAL AREAS

Taking the developments described in this study, together with more general information relating to the city as a whole, what speculations may be ventured regarding the future racial composition of Philadelphia's residential areas? Does the evidence indicate that all areas in the city and suburbs will eventually become mixed, or do the data suggest a continuation of the segregated patterns of the past?

The study by itself reveals conflicting tendencies, the net effects of which cannot be evaluated without considering a number of additional factors. On the one hand, Negroes were able to purchase homes not only on equal terms with whites, but more importantly, in areas which until very recently had been closed to them. This was true not only in the areas chosen for study but in many other sections of the city as well. In addition, a significant number of white families continued to purchase homes in areas which were mixed or showed indications of becoming mixed in the immediate future. These facts considered by themselves would support the conclusion that the Negro population will gradually be dispersed throughout a large number of residential areas in the city, and while some whites will tend to leave these areas, others will stay, and still others will move in. Thus, stable mixed areas would become the typical pattern.

The contrary tendencies, however, must also be examined. Although many whites living in predominantly white sections of mixed areas had no objections to or even awareness of the small percentage of Negroes nearby, when this percentage was exceeded and the trend in sales indicated that the proportion of Negroes would continue to increase, many white residents chose to move to other areas. At the same time, the number of whites who purchased in the areas fell very sharply. Although the data are by no means conclusive, they suggest that the threshold is rather low, perhaps much lower than the proportion of Negroes in the population of the city. Thus, although a hard core of whites might remain and a few more move to the area for a variety of reasons, the prospect is that the proportion of Negroes in such areas will gradually increase. If this is the typical case, it implies a pattern of predominantly Negro communities interspersed throughout the city.

A number of additional factors are crucial in determining whether a pattern of concentration or dispersion will, in fact, emerge. Although new areas will become available to Negroes, some will be entered more readily than others, and there will undoubtedly be a tendency for nonwhites to purchase in areas that already have been entered. In the areas investigated in this study, the spread of Negro population occurred basically on the edges of existing concentrations despite the fact that some larger jumps were observed.

The tendency to move to areas in which Negroes are already in residence is due in part to the desire to obtain satisfactory housing without the risk of rebuff and in part to a positive desire to live in an area in which there is an appreciable number of other Negroes.

This phenomenon has been observed among other ethnic groups such as Jews and Italians who attach considerable value to the comfort and ease of communication with people of like culture and heritage. As the housing shortage for Negroes eases, non-whites may lack the incentive to pioneer their way into new areas. Thus, although segregation may disappear, congregation may not.

A continuation of the present nonwhite nodes is to be expected on other grounds as well. Although rising incomes and increased market freedom may enable many nonwhite families to leave the ghettos, the racial composition of existing Negro communities will remain unchanged, for it is not likely that white families can be attracted to them. Such an occurrence would be counter to virtually all past experience and cannot be expected until urban renewal programs materially alter existing nonwhite residential areas.

But what about the fringe areas? Will there be bands of stable mixed neighborhoods extending for miles around nonwhite nodes or will the mixed peripheral zones separating Negro and white areas be narrowly restricted? Again we must go somewhat beyond the findings of the study and examine other relevant factors. Many whites who wish to move from mixed neighborhoods may be prevented from doing so because equivalent houses are not available in acceptable all-white areas at prices they can afford to pay. Their housing alternatives will be closely related to the relative size of Negro demand. Although Negroes comprise one-quarter of the total population in Philadelphia, they constitute more than one-third of the group with incomes less than $4,000 and only 10 percent of those with incomes in excess of $6,000. Thus, Negro-white competition for housing will be concentrated to a large extent in price ranges below the minimum for new construction. Demand from these groups, therefore, will be limited to moderate-priced units in the existing stock.

Consequently, many whites in the lower-middle-income groups who might prefer to move from mixed areas will have a diminishing number of all-white neighborhoods available to them and, as a result, rapid change in neighborhood composition will be inhibited. Moreover, if pending legislation is enacted requiring home builders, and perhaps owners of existing housing and real estate brokers as well, to pursue a policy of nondiscrimination, the incentive for whites to move from existing mixed areas may be greatly reduced as alternative opportunities disappear. Thus, stable mixed areas may emerge as a general pattern in those sections of the city in which moderately priced homes are located. In higher-income areas, where the proportion of Negro demanders is very small, there will be a greater likelihood that a white family will be able to purchase a home in an all-white area. Even if some Negroes in this income bracket do not choose to live among nonwhites, this sector of the housing market will be almost entirely white.

Of all the factors that will determine the ultimate racial composition of our urban areas, perhaps attitudes are most important. It has been noted that many whites did not think of themselves as living in mixed areas even though they knew there were Negroes only a block away. This may well be a precursor to a more pervasive change in attitude. There is little doubt that both whites and Negroes have improved their view of each other over the past decades and that the present trend in the direction of social and economic equality for Negroes will continue unabated. With widening educational opportunities and opening of new occupational lines, differences between whites and nonwhites will diminish. As this time approaches, perhaps men will be more and more inclined to choose their neighbors on the basis of their essential worth and not according to the color of their skin.

Appendices

Racial Transition in an Upper Income Area: West Mount Airy, Philadelphia

Germantown, with its broad, tree-lined streets and stately mansions surrounded by extensive lawns and gardens, has always been one of Philadelphia's most favored residential areas. Founded in 1683 by a band of Dutch Mennonite immigrants, it soon became a residential center for this continental Quaker group from whom the name "Germantown" was erroneously derived. The industrious new settlers grew both in numbers and in wealth, and over the years the area attracted many well-to-do families of other faiths. By the end of the eighteenth century, residence in the area came to signify quiet and gracious living, a reputation that it holds to this day.

Germantown has been called Philadelphia's first restricted real estate development.[1] In the latter part of the colonial period, prospective settlers in the area could buy property only upon the recommendation and approval of the local residents. Even visits of short duration were regulated, for inns in the neighborhood were prohibited from providing overnight accommodations to guests unless they held appropriate letters of introduction.

Today, some of the old landmarks have disappeared, replaced

---

[1] Struthers Burt, *Philadelphia, Holy Experiment* (London: Rich and Cowan, 1947), p. 53.

by groups of row houses and multistory apartments. Although the area has lost much of its homogeneity, many of the original social and physical characteristics of the area still persist. In general, the appearance of the neighborhood offers a pleasing contrast to the monotonous succession of row houses characteristic of many other areas of the city, for in Germantown, the prevailing type of structure is still the large, detached or semidetached single-family unit.

Like many other neighborhoods in Philadelphia, parts of Germantown are in the process of racial transition. For years there have been Negro families living in a few of the Germantown neighborhoods, but since 1950, additional nonwhite households have been entering other sections of the area in modest but increasing numbers. As in other neighborhoods, the entry of Negro homeowners into Germantown has created problems of social adjustment, both for the incoming Negro and for the white residents.

The pattern of Negro migration into this area is unique for Philadelphia, for some of it has occurred in West Mount Airy, the only upper-class white neighborhood in the city in which Negroes have purchased homes in appreciable numbers. Because of the many differences between the experiences of West Mount Airy and those of the four areas reported in the body of this monograph, it was felt an analysis of this area would be of particular value in interpreting our findings and in giving balance to the study. Although time and resources did not permit the same scale of research, it was possible to obtain for part of the West Mount Airy neighborhood detailed information concerning each home purchase in the area beginning with the year prior to the first Negro entry. This presented a rare opportunity to study the pattern of racial transition in an established upper-class neighborhood and its effect upon the local market for residential real estate.

The study of West Mount Airy was addressed to the following questions: (1) Did the Negro entrants tend to cluster or did they locate without pattern? (2) Did the spatial distribution of the new entrants have any effect on the spatial distribution of established and prospective white residents in the area? (3) Were the financial arrangements attendant upon the purchase of homes more or less favorable for Negroes than for whites? (4) What happened to house prices in the area? (5) What factors governed the rate and pattern of racial transition? (6) How did the white residents react to the entry of Negroes? (7) What happened to white purchases in the area as a result of the entry of Negroes? (8) Finally, what are the prospects for the establishment of a stable, biracial pattern in the community, i.e., will the process of transition continue until the neighborhood is predominantly Negro or will it stop at an earlier stage?

DESCRIPTION OF THE STUDY AREA

The portion of West Mount Airy selected for this study is a wedge-shaped zone of 41 residential blocks. It is bounded by Wissahickon Avenue on the west, Ellet Street on the north, the Chestnut Hill line of the Pennsylvania Railroad on the east, and Johnson Street on the south. In this area there are roughly 800

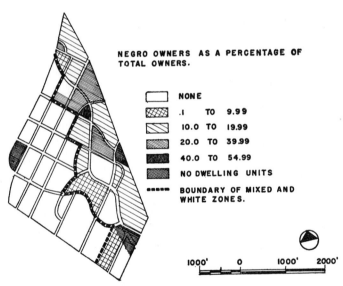

Fig. A-1. Negro ownership of single-family homes, West Mount Airy, 1955.

single- and two-family dwellings, ranging in age from 30 to 100 years and in value from $6,000 to $100,000. In 1950, their average value was approximately $17,000 with most of the units falling into the $12,000 to $30,000 bracket.[2] At the time of the 1950 Census, a few Negro residents were located on the other side of the railroad line, and a minor concentration of nonwhite families was to be found in lower-priced houses several blocks away in the vicinity of Germantown Avenue.

NUMBER AND SPATIAL DISTRIBUTION OF NEGRO AND WHITE BUYERS

The first Negro entry in the West Mount Airy neighborhood departed from the usual pattern of expansion from the periphery of a concentration of nonwhites. The existence of an established Neparture of whites in the expectation of Negro entry, nor was there gro community on the edge of an all-white area frequently causes whites to move in anticipation of the entry of Negroes into the area. Houses become difficult to sell to other white families and, as a consequence, the entrance of Negro families is facilitated.

This was not the case in West Mount Airy. There was no deany diminution of demand for that reason. Negro entry was, however, assisted by a softening of the market. For a period of several years, the larger and older homes which were expensive to operate and difficult to maintain had been put up for sale at a rate in excess of that which the market could absorb at existing price levels. It was in response to this situation that the first Negro family purchased a home for owner-occupancy in West Mount Airy in January, 1951.

The second nonwhite acquisition did not take place until more than a year later. Thereafter, the number of Negro purchasers increased markedly, reaching a high of eighteen in 1954, and by the end of 1955 a total of forty-six nonwhite families had purchased in the area.

From 1951 to 1953, Negro purchases were concentrated in two separate clusters roughly four blocks apart along Lincoln Drive. In 1954 and 1955, the area of Negro in-migration expanded to form a contiguous zone of eighteen mixed blocks including nearly every block adjoining Lincoln Drive. Each year an increasing

---

[2] Current house values were estimated from field inquiries. Value data for 1950, however, are from *U. S. Census of Housing: 1950*, vol. V, *Block Statistics*, part 143, "Philadelphia," table 3.

number of additional street fronts were entered by Negroes reaching a peak of seven in 1954. In the following year, the number fell to two, perhaps because later Negro in-migrants preferred street fronts already entered or because a relatively larger number of dwellings were for sale on such street fronts, or both.

By the end of 1955, Negro families owned 20 to 55 percent of the houses in six of the blocks located in the northern half of the area. In an additional seven blocks they constituted 10 to 20 percent of the total, and in five blocks, they were in possession of less than 10 percent of the homes. In twenty-three of the forty-one blocks there were no Negro residents at all.

From 1950 through 1955, 194 white families acquired homes in the study area. The overwhelming majority of the white buyers in every year since 1951 bought into the predominantly white sections of the area, despite the growing proportion of mixed blocks. This tendency was revealed by an examination of the effect of Negro in-migration on subsequent white purchases in a twenty-two block "mixed zone." This zone was delimited to include the eighteen contiguous blocks which were mixed in 1955, together with four all-white blocks which were bounded on at least three sides by mixed blocks.

In 1950, the year prior to the arrival of the first Negro family in West Mount Airy, twenty-three whites bought homes in the mixed zone. Between 1953 and 1955 when the volume of Negro in-migration increased, there was a marked inverse correlation between the number of white purchases and the proportion of Negro residents in the zone, i.e., the number of white buyers fell each year as the proportion of Negroes in the total population increased. In 1954, the number of Negro buyers exceeded the number of white buyers for the first time; and in 1955 only six whites compared with sixteen Negroes bought in the zone.

CHARACTERISTICS OF NEW ENTRANTS

It is commonly assumed that the social and economic characteristics of incoming Negroes may influence the housing-market behavior of white residents. Other things being equal, if the social and economic status of Negro in-migrants is the same or higher than that of existing residents, net out-migration of the latter may be less than it would be were the Negroes from a lower stratum of society. Judging from the occupations of a sample of 1954 and 1955 nonwhite purchasers, it appears that they enjoyed satisfactory incomes and at least moderate wealth and social status. With one exception, all were professional men—physicians, dentists, teachers, or employed in other technical or professional capacities. Thus, the new Negro arrivals were persons of education and professional attainment and in this regard undoubtedly compared very favorably with the resident population.

PRICE LEVELS AND TRENDS

The average prices of homes sold in the study area showed very little change during the period 1950 to 1953, standing slightly above $17,000 in each of these years. In 1954, the average selling price dipped to $16,500 and the following year declined further to $14,800. In addition to variations over time, there were also substantial differences between prices in the mixed zone and in the white zone. In the former area, average prices paid for the properties that changed hands in the years 1950 to 1953 ranged between $18,900 and $20,300; in 1954 the mean transfer figure was only $17,800, and in 1955 it stood at $17,400. Average prices in the white zone were $3,000 to $6,000 less than those in the mixed zone throughout the entire 1950–1955 period. In the white zone, prices rose from $14,250 in 1950 to $15,500 in 1952 and then declined to a low of $12,250 in 1955.

In each year the average selling price of houses in the study area was less than the average value ($18,000) of all single-family owner-occupied structures in the area as reported in the 1950 Census. This relationship was observed in both the white and the mixed zones where the 1950 average values were $16,890 and $20,545, respectively. An examination of the sales revealed that structures of high quality were transferred less frequently than the remainder of the stock. This fact in itself could account for at least some of the difference. In addition, in view of the reported weakening of demand from 1946 to 1950, it is likely that many of the owners, since they were not in daily contact with the market, may have reported values in 1950 that reflected the price situation that prevailed in the years prior to the easing of the housing shortage.

There is a suggestion in the price figures of a continuation of the market softening which began prior to 1950. The extent to which there was an actual downward shift in the level of prices of comparable homes, however, cannot be measured without holding quality constant. This has been done in a rough fashion by the use of sales price to assessed value ratios.[3] The ratios suggest a generally upward price movement in both zones from 1950 to 1953 and then a reversal of the trend through 1955. The random fluctuations about the means of these ratios are so large, however, and the number of observations are so small, that any evaluation of price trends from sales data alone is difficult and should be accepted with caution.[4]

There is another bit of evidence that tends to support the impression that house prices moved downward after 1952. Limited information drawn from the Germantown Multiple Listing Service records points to a weakening in the housing market in West Mount Airy in 1952–1953, the years of accelerated Negro entry into the area. According to these records, the median ratio of sale price to asking price for the 38 West Mount Airy properties listed during 1952 to 1954—the only years for which there is information—fell substantially during 1952 and 1953. In the next year, however, there was little change in the ratio. The files show, too, that elapsed time between listing and sale rose sharply from 1953 to the end of 1954, another indication of decline in demand. This experience, however, was typical of the city as a whole.

Available statistics, therefore, indicate that there may have been a moderate decline in prices in West Mount Airy subsequent to entry by Negro families. This is in marked contrast with the situation in various other sections of the city where average sale prices have tended to rise following the influx of Negroes.

---

[3] For a discussion of the limitations of the sales price-assessed value ratio for comparisons of this sort, see Appendix C.

[4] It may be noted that sales price-assessed value ratios in the white zone were consistently higher than the ratios in the mixed zone, but whether this represents better housing buys in the mixed zone or variations in assessment practices according to house value is not known.

Comparison of prices paid by Negro and white buyers.—The mean prices paid for houses by Negroes entering West Mount Airy in 1953, 1954, and 1955, the only years for which the number of sales was sufficient to justify comparisons, were several thousand dollars higher than the prices paid by their white counterparts. This does not mean that sellers discriminated against Negro buyers. On the contrary, it is a reflection of the fact that colored families gravitated toward homes of better quality. Within the mixed zone, whites and Negroes paid roughly the same prices.[5] For the period 1953 to 1955, the mean sales figure for homes acquired in this zone by nonwhite families was $17,990, whereas the corresponding figure for white purchases was $18,350. The average SP–AV ratios for the two groups were also almost identical, 1.43 and 1.45, respectively.

MORTGAGE TERMS

In the other mixed neighborhoods which we studied, mortgage lenders pursued a policy of extending favorable terms to their new customers, evidently with the view of capturing as much as possible of the growing Negro market. In West Mount Airy, however, the evidence suggests that Negroes as a group received decidedly less favorable mortgage terms than did whites. In 1953, 1954, and 1955,[6] 70 percent of the white families obtaining mortgages were granted interest rates of less than 5 percent, while only 24 percent of the Negro mortgagors fell into this category. There were similar differences in loan-to-value ratios: loans which represented 90 percent or more of the purchase price were granted to ten of eighty-three whites as against none of forty-two Negroes. Over the three-year period, the median loan to value ratio of white acquisitions was 74 percent and of Negro purchases 69 percent.

Although these fragments of information reveal that Negro

---

[5] Possible exceptions to this statement were the first Negro entrants on all-white street fronts who may have paid somewhat higher prices than whites and other Negroes who purchased comparable structures. The data on this question, however, are by no means conclusive.

[6] Comparisons are made only for these three years because until 1953 there were an insufficient number of Negro purchases to examine statistically. Even in 1953, nonwhite acquisitions were perhaps too few to permit satisfactory comparisons.

borrowers were required to make larger down payments and pay higher interest charges, these differences may be attributable to circumstances completely unrelated to race.

First, and most important, down payment differences may be partially explained by the fact that bankers customarily lower the loan to value ratio as price rises. Or, in other words, a mortgage will typically represent a smaller proportion of price on a $30,000 home than on a $10,000 dwelling and this is true for conventional loans as well as for FHA and VA mortgages. It was noted earlier that most Negroes entering West Mount Airy from 1951 to 1955 bought homes priced at $14,000 or more, while most whites, on the other hand, purchased homes that sold for less than that sum. This by itself could account for the less favorable terms obtained by Negroes. It is relevant, too, that the two white buyers who obtained 100 percent mortgages bought homes priced between $10,000 and $12,000, and seven of the eight whites whose loan-value ratios were 90 percent or more paid less than $16,000 for their new homes.

Secondly, several informed persons in the locality suggested that few if any Negroes, in contrast to the white buyers, were eligible for VA loans. This fact, if true, would also explain a major part of the differences in mortgage terms.

A third and final reason for the differences between terms received by Negroes and whites relates to the sources of mortgage funds, for there is considerable variation in the lending policies and practices among financial institutions. Nearly half (46 percent) of the white buyers were accommodated by mutual savings banks and another one-fourth (27 percent) by savings and loan associations. Sixty-five percent of the Negro acquisitions were mortgaged by savings and loan associations, and only 18 percent by mutual savings fund societies. When interest rates and down payments for whites and Negro families were standardized by type of lender, much of the difference was explained.

These facts alone do not deny the existence of discrimination for it is, of course, possible that Negroes had difficulty in obtaining loans from the institutions which granted more liberal terms.

Of the thirty-four institutions which made loans to home buyers during the period 1954 to 1955, only seven made loans to both

Negroes and whites. Fourteen granted mortgages to whites only, and thirteen to Negroes only. Most of these institutions, however, made only one or two loans each in the locality. Only eight lenders made three or more loans and six of these loaned to both Negroes and whites. The six included three mutual savings fund societies, and three savings and loan associations. In addition, one large central city commercial bank which advanced only two loans made one to a Negro and one to a white buyer. Thus, it does not appear that discrimination was practiced in the sense of unwillingness to make loans to Negroes.

The mortgages received by first Negro entrants were of special interest because it is often maintained that these families have particular difficulty obtaining loans and are, therefore, compelled to accept stringent terms. In West Mount Airy, however, the mortgage terms obtained by first Negro entrants into a street front were generally comparable with those of other Negro buyers. Of the thirteen first entrants who obtained mortgages, four obtained loans carrying an interest rate of 4.5 percent, and five paid 6 percent or more. The loan–value ratio of all first-entrant mortgages varied between 50 percent and 83 percent. Seven placed their loans with savings and loan associations, two with a savings bank, and one with a central city bank; only three obtained their funds from private sources. Moreover, three of the first Negro entrants borrowed from lenders located in Germantown or mortgagees who had local offices in the area. In no case was a loan obtained from a Negro-managed lending institution. Thus, even among those Negro families who might have been expected to have the greatest difficulty in obtaining mortgage loans, there was general reliance on institutional sources of financing.

EFFECT OF NEGRO ENTRY ON MARKET ACTIVITY

It is frequently averred that the entrance of Negroes into an area will cause a steady exodus of whites, as in fact apparently occurred in West Philadelphia and Strawberry Mansion. In West Mount Airy, however, the out-migration of whites seems to have been prompted mainly by considerations other than unwillingness to live in a racially mixed neighborhood. Had Negro entry caused whites to leave, the turnover of dwelling units would have increased, adding those sales precipitated by the change in the area to the departures which normally occur.

Turnover rates in the mixed zone stayed at a relatively constant figure averaging over 6 percent per year, a rate approximately the same as that for the city as a whole during 1950 to 1955.[7] The turnover rates in the white zone were substantially less than those in the mixed zone, but they increased gradually with a minor interruption over the six-year period from 4 percent to 5.5 percent, suggesting a fairly strong market in that neighborhood.

THE EFFECT OF COMMUNITY ACTION

The absence of extensive turnover was in considerable measure the result of a concerted community effort directed toward this end. In 1953, in response to an increase in the number of homes placed on the market, an active campaign was initiated by community leaders to discourage homeowners from making hasty and ill-considered sales and to urge them to reappraise their responses to their new Negro neighbors. These efforts together with the unattractive price offers made by would-be buyers seem to have encouraged many to withdraw their properties from the market.

Organized community efforts directed toward a solution to the racial problem began in the spring of 1953 with the formation of the West Mount Airy Neighbors, an association created expressly to curb the departure of white residents from the area. Although this organization was extremely active during the next two years, its efforts were restricted to only a small portion of the area subject to racial change. These efforts were soon given a broader base when the pastors of the four major religious organizations in

---

[7] This would seem at variance with the statement made earlier that the prices for the more expensive houses were low even prior to Negro entry because of the slow turnover. Real estate brokers in the area, however, stated that the number of listings in the Lincoln Drive area in the period 1946 to 1950 was unusually high, whereas the proportion of these properties for which buyers were to be found was abnormally small. Since the effective supply consists of houses for sale, rather than all existing houses, a high rate of turnover expressed as a proportion of houses sold to total houses would, thus, be perfectly consistent under the above assumption with a sluggish market.

Mount Airy and the adjoining Pelham neighborhood[8] met to discuss the problems caused by Negro in-migration. The outgrowth of this and subsequent meetings was the formation of the Church Community Council of Pelham representing the members of three of the groups.[9] As the scope of the Council's activities expanded, its steering committee was progressively enlarged to include representatives of the West Mount Airy Neighbors, pastors from other churches, and members at large from the area, among whom were several prominent Negroes.

The Pelham Council drew up a broad program directed toward allaying popular fears of the consequences of racial transition, encouraging residents to accept the presence of Negroes in the neighborhood, and discouraging questionable practices among real estate agents. Some of the activities conducted by the Council included the circulation of petitions by residents protesting against such business practices as urging owners to sell because of the changing character of the neighborhood and the holding of a series of public meetings designed to familiarize residents with unfavorable consequences of panic selling. With the aid and support of the Philadelphia Fellowship Commission and the Philadelphia Real Estate Board the Council attempted to stop telephone and mail solicitation of a panic-generating character. It also fought to remove racial connotations from real estate advertising. All three participating churches were given awards by the Fellowship Commission in 1957 for their success in bringing about harmonious race relations in the area.

FUTURE OF THE AREA

Since 1951, the year of the initial nonwhite entry, the Negro population of West Mount Airy has continued to rise while the number of whites entering the area and the total white population have diminished. This does not, however, imply that the transition now under way will proceed until the neighborhood is largely Negro. A number of factors militate against an increase in the rate of racial

---

[8] The Unitarian Church of Germantown, the Germantown Jewish Center, the Epiphany Episcopal Church, the Summit Presbyterian Church.
[9] The Summit Presbyterian Church congregation voted against joining the Council.

displacement in West Mount Airy and may, in fact, serve to stabilize the racial character of the area:

1. The existing Negro population is a relatively small part of the total population in the area. It is widely thought that the extent of concentration of Negroes in a neighborhood is as important as the rate of Negro in-migration in affecting the rate of net white out-migration. Many whites who would not object to the presence of two or three colored families in their immediate vicinity, will flee or refuse to enter an area if the proportion of Negroes reaches a level which in their opinion is too high. On this score, the situation in West Mount Airy at the end of 1955 was favorable to continued biracial occupancy. Only 14 percent of the families in the mixed section of the area and a much lower proportion in the area as a whole were Negro.

2. There is no established all-Negro neighborhood in the immediate vicinity and, therefore, out-migration may be expected to take place at a slow rate if at all. Moreover, white buyers may be less reluctant to purchase in an area with a small proportion of Negroes if they have reason to believe that the proportion will remain small. This attitude is strengthened if the Negro residents do not represent the outermost fringe of a large and expanding Negro neighborhood.

3. The predominance of detached dwelling units tends to make contact among neighbors volitional rather than inevitable. In West Mount Airy the typical single-family home is detached and located on a large-sized lot with shade trees and bushes and shrubs. Many houses are on top of an incline, some distance from the street. Thus, the close daily contact which is almost unavoidable in adjoining row houses is greatly reduced when houses are widely spaced and screened from each other and from the passers-by.

4. Relatively few Negroes in the Philadelphia area have incomes large enough to purchase dwellings in West Mount Airy at the prevailing level of prices. No doubt, if all Negroes with high incomes chose to live in West Mount Airy, the area would indeed become predominantly nonwhite, but this possibility is highly unlikely.

5. The high social and occupational status of the Negro families makes them in every objective sense eminently desirable members of the community and facilitates their acceptance both by white residents and by potential white purchasers.

6. The attitudes of the white residents are moderately sympathetic and the neighborhood organizations promoting stability are strong and effective. These organizations have not only been able to prevent much panic selling, but they have also succeeded in attracting white families to the area.

Although the observations above point to a conclusion that racial displacement in West Mount Airy will proceed at a moderate rate, they do not reveal the point in time at which displacement will cease completely nor what the racial characteristics of the area will be at that time. Cessation of transition can occur only when white in-migration equals white out-migration. In the mixed zone, this balance may never be fully achieved. The increase in the proportion of Negroes entering the mixed zone has been accompanied by a reduction in the number of white families entering the area, so that at present most of the mixed blocks and virtually all of the mixed street fronts in the zone are shunned by white buyers.

In the white zone, on the other hand, the best prediction may be described as an informed guess. It is conceivable that Negro entry into a major portion of the white zone may never occur, for the expansion of the area which is already slowing down can proceed in three other directions; it need not move westward. Finally, nonwhite entry into the white zone if it takes place at all may not occur for a number of years by which time white families will have grown accustomed to Negro neighborhoods, and increased market freedom will enable Negroes to choose houses in many sections of the city.

When Negroes Came to Clearview

This appendix describes some of the events leading up to Negro entry into an all-white block in a middle-income Philadelphia neighborhood.[1] They were observed by one of the authors on what was intended to be a routine research visit.

Clearview Avenue is located in the Germantown section of Philadelphia four blocks north of 6800 Germantown Avenue. It is a street one block in length fronted by twenty-eight row houses of roughly $7,000 to $7,800 in value. A large proportion of the residents of Clearview, like those in nearby blocks, are Irish Catholics and constitute a rather closely knit group.

In 1952 a development of row houses was built on Pleasant Avenue one block north of Clearview Avenue. Negro families soon occupied the new development and other nearby blocks. None came as far south as Clearview, however, and there was no contact with Negroes over the back fence because a playground separated the houses on Clearview from those on Pleasant. Nevertheless, a "threat" existed in the minds of Clearview residents.

---

[1] For another example of a similar incident, see "Story of a 'Busted Block'," *Philadelphia Evening Bulletin,* January 24, 1954, reprinted in William B. Dickinson, *This is Greater Philadelphia* (Philadelphia: The Bulletin Company, 1954).

They had often discussed the matter assuring one another that they would not sell to Negroes. The possibility of Negro entry may also have occurred to potential buyers, for sales were slow and prices dropped about $500 during this period. The price decline, however, was sufficient to attract a few white purchasers, and in 1955 there were five acquisitions.

Late in 1955 a real estate salesman told one of the residents in the block that he could sell her home for about $8,200. Encouraged by this promise, the owner purchased a home in another area only to find that the salesman could not deliver a buyer for any price over $6,800. The owner withheld a decision to sell at so low a price, but when several months had passed without a buyer, she grew increasingly concerned because she had extended her resources to the limit in purchasing the second house. In February, 1956, she was informed that a Negro family was interested in her house and was prepared to pay over $7,000. After weighing the matter for a short time, she told one of her neighbors about the offer. Her choice, she said, was either to lose her friends or her money, and she was afraid it would have to be her friends. On February 28, 1957, she entered into an agreement of sale for $7,450, and thus the transition began.

From then on events moved rapidly. The following morning real estate salesmen were out contacting all homeowners in the block, and by midafternoon a number of the residents had decided to sell. A local real estate broker (a good friend of several of the residents) who had not solicited any listings in the block was asked by four owners to list their homes.

One of the owners, a housewife, came into the realty office personally to make this request. Her remarks, quoted verbatim, vividly demonstrate the fears which are often caused by Negro entry.

"I don't know where we'll go, but we're going."

"Jack and I could stand it, but we're not going to expose our kids to it."

"Mrs. _____ said she was going to stay if every last house was sold to Negroes, and she breaks the block. Boy, there is going to be another case for the jury."

"It's not the best class of colored moving in, you know."

"It wouldn't be so bad, but the houses are too darn close together."

"We may not be able to escape forever, but we'll try for a while."

"Now look, we're going to sell. If you don't want the listing, we'll go to someone else, but we thought we would give you first chance at it."

"Prices won't go back up; they'll keep going down."[2]

"We talked about a farm, and Janet [the daughter] has already asked if she could have a collie."

The family evidently had not only talked about a farm, but had found two newspaper listings which they intended to investigate. In less than twenty-four hours, their whole life had been changed radically because of an innocent purchase by a single nonwhite family.

The extent to which panic was generated by the real estate salesmen and the extent to which it would have developed in any event cannot be determined. It could be reasoned that the undercurrents of panic had been in motion for years waiting to come to the surface. The purchase viewed as a violation of the sanctity of the block may have been the only event necessary to precipitate the ensuing hysteria.

In his conversations with the distressed housewife and with the other homeowners with whom he spoke over the phone, the broker tried to dispel their fears, even though this obviously meant a reduction in his potential income. He advised them that it was foolish to sell; that one Negro would not hurt a block; that the owners would take a serious financial loss were they to sell now, but that if they waited prices would not fall; that there was no sense in fleeing from Negroes because in a few years there would be nonwhites in every neighborhood anyway; and that nowhere else was there as good a house available for the same money.

The broker managed to dissuade two of the would-be sellers,

---

[2] The remarks are presented roughly in the order in which they were made. It is interesting that the argument that prices would go down was one of the last objections raised by the lady. Although it is not revealed in the statements presented here, her principal fear seemed to stem from a firm conviction that the block would soon be all Negro.

and apparently panic subsided among most of the other owners because only two "For Sale" signs were in evidence on the block a week later. By December, however, four additional Negro families had purchased homes at prices ranging from $7,400 to $7,900. Within a year transition was well under way.

Research Methods and Sources of Data

THE SELECTION OF STUDY AREAS

In selecting areas for study we were confronted with a series of problems. What precisely is meant by a mixed area? Did we want the study areas to be, and could they be, representative of all areas of their type in the city or were there special considerations that dictated a choice of areas that possessed particular characteristics? How were the exact boundaries to be determined?

Strictly speaking, an area is mixed if it contains anything less than a solid concentration of either Negroes or whites. Quite obviously, the residence of one or a few racially atypical families is not sufficient to alter the predominant characteristic of the area. If the area is equally divided racially, then its mixture is beyond dispute. But there is some point between zero and 50 percent at which the size of the minority, be it white or Negro, will cause the area to be viewed as mixed. For some, as little as 5 percent will be sufficient, although for others ratios as high as 25 or 30 percent are required. This, in a sense, is the problem of determining how many hairs make a beard.

The final decision was dictated by the objective of the study, although the precise limits were set arbitrarily. Since it was proposed to study the influence of mixed occupancy on potential housing demand, the relative proportions of whites and nonwhites had to be such that families in each color group were likely to be found in the home-purchase market and where the color issue could not be disregarded. To our minds at this stage of the research this meant that the racially mixed areas eligible for investigation were those in which the nonwhites were socially visible, but were still in the minority. Translated into numerical terms for purposes of this study, we decided to select areas in which the nonwhite population fell between 10 and 50 percent of the total.

It was felt that the areas selected for study should not include those in which the family incomes were too low or too high, or districts where rental was the prevalent type of tenure. The sphere of consideration was thus narrowed to include mixed areas where the incomes of the population fell in the middle ranges and where the single-family dwelling occupied by the owner predominated.

Because mixed areas are usually associated with districts undergoing transition, and because some transitional areas are on the downgrade or have reached a slum state, it was necessary to separate these elements in considering the areas to be selected for study. Preliminary inspection revealed that there were wide differences among the eligible mixed areas both in the rapidity of transition and in the quality of the existing housing supply. Both of these factors are of no little relevance in market analysis. The speed of transition not only implies change in the color composition of the population, but it is usually accompanied by a higher than average rate of transactions and uncertainty regarding the future. The quality of housing in an area is not necessarily related to the rate of transition, but may be associated with the conditions under which transition occurs. During periods of rising incomes and upward social mobility, white families, in an attempt to increase their living standards, will voluntarily leave areas in order to improve the quality of their housing, and thus the entrance of new groups if not welcomed is at least not strongly resisted. In areas in which the quality of housing is acceptable or good, the incentive to leave is diminished and the lack of available houses for newcomers augments the complexity of the competition for space.

In this study it was not felt necessary to stipulate the rapidity of transition and the quality of the housing stock as formal variables and to relate them to equally formal hypotheses. In our work the major purposes were served by a less rigorous approach. In deciding to select areas that differed in rate of transition and in the quality of the housing stock, we were more concerned about obtaining a variety of situations and possessing a foreknowledge of the existence and dimension of the factors that might have market relevance. To economize in the study design, we decided to choose four areas and double up on their characteristics. Thus, in two of the four, transition was more rapid and in the remaining two the change was proceeding at a slower pace. In each pair of areas thus selected, one was marked by housing of poor quality and one possessed dwelling units of acceptable standard.

The next problem was to determine the criteria for the selection of the boundaries of each of the study areas. Ideally the areas should encompass a complete neighborhood or a so-called natural area. But what neighborhood should be chosen? Is it one that conforms with images of individuals or one that can be delineated by ecological or market-area concepts, limited though they be for this purpose? Is it the area that includes the park and the church and the grocery store, or does it also include the school, the community center, the movie houses, and the shopping districts that are part of the life of the family with growing children? Should all portions of the area be within comfortable walking distance or should a larger radius be considered?

These questions came up time and time again in the area selection. Despite attempts to utilize neighborhood and market-area concepts in defining study areas, both concepts had to be partially abandoned in favor of the use of census tracts to delineate boundaries. The ponderous body of data organized into these statistical units virtually dictates their use if any historical comparisons are to be made and if the task of future research workers is to be facilitated. We made certain that the tract boundaries did not do violence to an area by not including an entire tract if it contained no more than a trivial section of the neighborhood. Thus, the study areas consisted of an integral number of tracts ranging as it turned out from one to eight.

In settling on the specific areas to be studied, a number of steps were required. First, every ward in the city was analyzed and a preliminary selection made of those that were likely to contain suitable census tracts. Then all tracts were examined in each of the wards that were chosen and a preliminary group of areas was selected. These areas and their boundaries were then carefully scrutinized by a group of experts, and on the basis of their advice a final determination was made.

The ward in Philadelphia is considerably larger than the census tract and, thus, provided a simplified means of approaching the first stage of the process of selection. Because of their size they are usually close to "natural" areas or the likelihood is greater that one or more will be contained within their boundaries. Nine wards were found in which the proportion of nonwhite population was between 10 and 30 percent. Some of the salient population and housing characteristics of these wards were then studied including the rate of change of nonwhite population and its relationship to the change in the total number of inhabitants, the change in occupancy by race, the condition of houses, the extent of overcrowding, etc. As a result of this examination five wards, two of which were contiguous, were subjected to further study.

At this point, the ward was abandoned as the unit of analysis. Not only did the wards encompass too large an area for the type of study that was contemplated, but also there were indications that the areas which conformed to our previously established criteria either straddled ward boundaries or were smaller than wards.

Each tract in the wards that were selected was then analyzed, plus the tracts that bordered these wards. Tracts where median income fell below $1,500 or where the proportion of nonwhite-occupied dwelling units was above 50 percent were eliminated unless they were completely surrounded by acceptable tracts. The population and housing characteristics of the remaining tracts were converted to indices and additional tracts were culled if their relative rank did not conform with the quality level of their area; that is, all tracts in the better quality–fast change areas had to rank higher than all tracts in the poorer quality–fast change areas, and better quality–slow change had to be above poorer quality-slow change. The following census categories of housing characteristics in 1950 were examined: median number of persons per dwelling unit, proportion of dwelling units with more than 1.01 persons per room, median value of one dwelling unit structures, median contract monthly rent, median income, population per household, proportion of units which were dilapidated or lacked private bath. On the basis of these characteristics, four groups of tracts were chosen in this step in the selection of areas for study.

The aid of persons thoroughly familiar with racial change and housing characteristics of the residential sections of Philadelphia was solicited at this point. They presented their appraisal of the study design and of the suitability of the areas that had been selected on the basis of census statistics and casual field inspection. These individuals provided qualitative information of an order not generally available in published documents as well as information on changes that had occurred since 1950.

Although the group suggested many additional criteria for the selection of areas—such as amicable race relations, equal distance from center of city, equal housing age, and several others—it was finally agreed that standardization along these lines would not be feasible, however desirable, since areas meeting our requirements with regard to proportion of nonwhites, rate of racial change, and housing quality were indeed rare.

The group accepted the two areas of slow change with little qualification. They pointed out, however, that one area of fast change where housing was of satisfactory quality in 1950 had begun to deteriorate some years earlier and would more suitably be considered as a poor-quality area today. In its place the group suggested, and we accepted, a fast change–better quality area in which only 2 percent of the dwelling units were occupied by nonwhites in 1950, but in 1955 contained an estimated nonwhite population of at least 15 percent.

PROPERTY TRANSFER DATA

Source and collection.—The data on property transfers were obtained from a private publication, the Philadelphia Real Estate Directory. Information in the directory is obtained by the publishers directly from the public records and also from local abstract companies. In some states and localities, records of real estate transfers are suspect because parties to the transactions often conceal the amount of the consideration. Pennsylvania law, however, requires that buyer and seller swear to the accuracy of the statement in the conveyance instrument and the opinion of practitioners is that the records of transactions in recent years are quite accurate. The directory itself also has a reputation for being accurate and is used by local, state, and federal agencies as well as by private businesses. It was possible by means of personal interviews with home purchasers in the study area to check the accuracy of some of the data contained in the directory and very few errors were uncovered.

Virtually every important transfer datum except mortgage amortization period appears in the directory. Included are:

1. Address of property
2. Name of owner
3. Address of owner
4. Date of deed recordation
5. Name of mortgagee
6. Address of mortgagee
7. Original amount of mortgage
8. Mortgage interest rate
9. Consideration
10. Assessed value
11. Lot size
12. Name of previous owner
13. Address of previous owner at time of transfer
14. Consideration paid by previous owner.

Symbols were used to identify mortgages covering more than one property, properties transferred subject to an existing mortgage, sheriff sales, and other special types of conveyances.

Data on all transfers within the study area in 1955 were transcribed from the directory to specially prepared property transfer cards. Of the 3,355 conveyances transcribed, a total of 1,015 were culled because they did not involve the bona fide transfer of a single-family home or because of some defect in identification. The initial culling process was performed as part of the transcription process and was then supplemented by a thorough field check.

About two-thirds of the rejections involved nominal considerations, transfers to clear title, transfers to heirs or to members of the same family, blanket sales covering more than one property, properties with wrong addresses, etc. A few sales involved strictly commercial, industrial, or institutional properties which were not of interest. A small portion of the transactions were sheriff sales. Their number was not sufficient to warrant a special analysis. The lack of such sales, however, was of some importance since an early study by the Philadelphia Housing Association suggested a causal relationship between racially changing neighborhoods and foreclosure rates.[1]

More than 10 percent of the rejected transactions involved structures containing more than one dwelling unit. Although the characteristics of these sales are important in understanding the nature of the market for investment in real property in the areas, they were excluded from this study of the market for owner-occupied dwellings. Because of the mixture of purposes in the acquisition of structures that contain a combination of residential and commercial space, over 200 properties of this type were also withdrawn from the analysis. Forty-one of these structures were purchased by whites, seventy-three by Negroes, and ninety by absentee owners.

Limitations of the data.—As in all studies, the data used to explore certain questions were deficient in one or more respects. The deficiencies were related both to the figures themselves and to the uses to which they were put. Fortunately, the data limitations did not impose insurmountable difficulties and are, therefore, discussed only briefly here.

a. *Lease-purchase agreements.*—Persons who wish to buy homes and who lack the cash to make a down payment sometimes finance the equity portion of the purchase price by renting the unit with the agreement that part of the rental payments will be applied toward the down payment. When the required amount of money has been accumulated, a mortgage is written for the balance of the consideration and title is transferred as in any ordinary transaction. This arrangement, termed a lease-purchase plan, has been criticized because it is sometimes consciously extended to individuals who are not expected to save the necessary amount of

[1] Bernard J. Newman, *Housing in Philadelphia, 1935* (Philadelphia Housing Association, 1936), p. 23.

money and who, thus, lose both the opportunity to acquire homes and their accumulated savings as well.

According to real estate brokers and mortgage lenders, some of the homes purchased in the study area in 1955 and in earlier years were originally acquired under previous lease-purchase agreements. These could not be identified from the records, however, and informed persons were not in agreement regarding their frequency. The inclusion of these transactions in the statistical summaries tends to distort the data because the amount of the down payment very often is excluded from the recorded purchase price and also because the recorded date of the sale lags behind the date when the actual process of acquisition began.

Of the white buyers who acquired homes in the study area in 1955, the maximum proportion who could have utilized this type of buying arrangement was estimated to be less than 10 percent. There are no data available, however, to aid in an estimation of how often the lease-purchase agreement was used by nonwhites. Ordinarily, this device might be expected to be found more frequently in the Negro market, but in the study area the observed differences in the white and nonwhite purchases were so few that it may perhaps be permissible to assume that the two groups of buyers were also similar with respect to their use of the lease-purchase instrument.

b. *Representativeness of the properties transferred.*—In this study all the bona fida home sales in the study areas were analyzed. The entire universe of sales was used primarily in order to obtain a sufficient number of white purchasers for an analysis in depth. This procedure also permitted an examination of the spatial distribution of white and nonwhite purchases and of mortgage lending activity.

The procedure, however, resulted in a sample that was not representative of the distribution of prices of all properties in the study areas. In West Philadelphia, for example, almost 50 percent of all transfers examined occurred in one small part of the area. Since there was a good deal of variation in the quality of homes among different parts of each study area, it is unlikely that the homes transferred were a cross section of all properties. The properties sold probably were an adequate sample, however, of the properties in subsections of the areas. Since much of the analysis was done on a subarea basis, the problem of representativeness was partially solved and additional refinement was, therefore, not attempted.

c. *Occupancy dates and recorded dates of sale.*—Since more ac-curate data were lacking, the recorded date of the sale was ac-cepted as the date of actual occupancy although this is not always true. In a few of the cases that were checked the time gap was several months. In most cases, however, the month of occupancy and the month of sale, as recorded, were identical. In the case of the first Negro family on the all-white block the actual date of the entry as well as the recorded date of sale was obtained because this identification was too important to be left to inference.

d. *Sales price–assessed value ratios.*—The 1955 sales prices of various groups of houses in the study area were related to their assessed values for the purpose of seeing whether Negroes paid more than whites for houses of comparable quality and whether houses in areas recently entered by Negroes brought higher prices than comparable houses in areas in the path of Negro expansion. Thus, the assessed values were used as a standard of comparability so that the prices of similar houses could be contrasted. It is not assumed that standardizing properties according to assessed values wipes out all causes of price variation except those being examined, nor is it assumed that this method is the best avenue of approaching the problem. With the available data it was the only approach and its limitations must be clearly recognized.

Sales prices of any two equally assessed residential properties in the same city may vary for a number of reasons:

1. Appraisals for tax purposes are not based on a thorough exam-ination of properties because it is impossible for the limited number of assessors to give each property individual attention. The appraisals, therefore, do not reflect all the quality differences among houses.

2. Included in sales prices may be a varying number of ap-pliances and installed equipment not reflected in the assessment figure.

3. The condition of the dwelling units may have changed in

different degree and direction subsequent to the most recent assessment. In Philadelphia the last general assessment was in 1947 and considerable change could have occurred since that time. There is some advantage, however, in having the old figures. The fact that the 1947 assessments were made prior to Negro entry into most parts of the study areas means that almost all of the valuations assigned do not reflect assessors' attitudes about Negroes.

4. Assessments in relation to market value may vary with price range.

5. The actual assessments are not all made by one individual and may differ for this reason, even though the general assessment procedures are the same.

6. There is considerable variation in the relative bargaining strength and market knowledge of buyers and sellers.

7. Terms of financing have an important bearing on sales prices.

Although it is obvious that because of these factors a comparison of sales price—assessed value ratios for any two houses would be of questionable value, it was felt that for large groups of houses the effects of these factors would cancel out and, therefore, make area and racial comparisons possible.

RACIAL IDENTIFICATION OF BUYERS, STREET FRONTS, AND BLOCKS

Letter carriers were engaged in their spare time to supply information on home buyers living on their routes. The carriers noted on each property transfer card whether the purchaser was an owner-occupant or absentee, and if the former, the racial designation. At the same time, the carriers noted whether the property was used exclusively as a single-family residence and whether the block and street front on which the purchase was made were white or mixed. Miscellaneous facts on vacancies, deaths, and the like were also provided.

This stage of the identification process also included a close examination of ancillary data compiled by the Philadelphia Housing Association and the Philadelphia Commission on Human Relations. Both of these groups maintained records of units available for Negro occupancy advertised in the local newspapers. If a property was advertised in one of the large metropolitan dailies as well as in one of the Negro papers, the block on which it was located was noted. Although the correlation between this type of information and actual Negro occupancy was not perfect, it was extremely good and constituted a major additional piece of preliminary data. The initial listing depended in some small measure on the 1950 *Census Block Statistics* for information on the early incidence of Negro occupancy. These data were of limited value not only because of the rapidity of change in some areas, but also because the 1950 statistics included Negro renters and an occasional Negro superintendent of large apartment houses.

The data furnished by the letter carriers and also much of the information obtained from the Real Estate Directory were verified by a field survey which included an inspection of blocks and street fronts. The racial identifications supplied by the letter carriers proved to be extremely accurate, but the interviewers did uncover numerous intrafamily transfers which were not apparent from the data in the Real Estate Directory or from other sources.

FIELD SURVEY OF BUYERS AND RENTERS

A structured field interview survey was conducted to ascertain the characteristics and motives of the purchasers as well as their attitudes toward and awareness of the mixed nature of their neighborhood. Interviews were conducted principally with white families who moved within one block of a Negro homeowner. Also interviewed were a sample of white renters and Negro purchasers, including among the latter a group that were the first homeowners on a previously all-white block.

Sample selection.—On the basis of the racial identification of buyers, street fronts, and blocks developed from information presented by letter carriers and from other sources described in the previous section, sampling frames were prepared for each of the relevant categories of potential respondents. The first compartment of persons interviewed consisted of white families who had purchased a single-family home for owner-occupancy in 1955 and who resided no more than a block away from a resident Negro homeowner. A complete listing was made of all families in this group and a 50 percent sample stratified by the density of Negro population in the zone of residence was drawn.

A second category consisted of white renter families living anywhere in the study areas. Interviews were limited to the residents of the larger apartment houses of better quality. A list was made of these structures and a sample devised. A large number of this group were difficult to contact and even their neighbors knew little about them. As a consequence, in the interest of economy, interviews were stopped when the total reached 100. It is because we were unable to evaluate the reliability of our sample of white renters that very little attention is devoted to this group in the study.

A third sample was drawn from a list of Negro owner-occupants in the study area. This sample constituted 15 percent of the entire category. In addition, a special effort was made to interview all Negro families who purchased homes on a previously all-white block in 1955.

The questionnaires.—Staff members and consultants experienced in problems of questionnaire design and problems of interracial housing devoted considerable effort to the construction and refinement of these instruments. Prior to pretest, questionnaire drafts were sent to local experts in the Philadelphia Commission on Human Relations, the Philadelphia Housing Association, the Redevelopment Authority, the office of the Housing Coördinator, the American Friends Service Committee, and several other organizations interested in housing and intergroup relations. Comments of these persons contributed materially to the final form of the questionnaires.

Renter and purchaser questionnaires differed very little in format and content. Most of the variation was related to the use of appropriate terminology such as "apartment" instead of "house" and "rent" instead of "monthly payments."

Demographic items on the questionnaire referred to household composition, place of birth, parents' places of birth, occupation and place of work of head of household, full-time secondary workers, monthly housing costs, total family income, religious preference, veteran status, and years of school completed. Length of time in house, in neighborhood, place of residence prior to moving to this neighborhood, and length of time in the Philadelphia Standard Metropolitan Area were established by another group of questions intended to supplement the demographic information.

Two questions dealt with reasons for choosing the specific area as a place of residence. Four more probed doubts about the decision to move and dissatisfactions with house or neighborhood. These were included to provide general opportunities for respondents to mention Negroes spontaneously.

Two questions concerning the presence of other ethnic groups in the neighborhood were in effect barrier items. If no prior mention of Negroes was made, these questions were then asked, and if the respondent still failed to mention Negroes, the racial attitude questions which followed were not asked.

For those respondents who mentioned Negroes, five groups of items probed racial attitude. One question was designed to determine the time at which respondents became aware of Negroes living in the neighborhood in relation to the time of the purchase decision and the time of actual occupancy. Another item dealt with social distance. Respondents were asked their feelings about owning a house in the same neighborhood with Negroes, on the same block, and next door. For renters a question was added regarding their feelings about renting in the same building with Negroes. Depending on the location of the home of the respondent, some of these questions related to direct experience, but for others they were purely speculative. Respondents were asked whether they wanted to stay in the area or leave or whether they were undecided. Those who wanted to leave or were undecided were asked if they were actively looking for another place to live. The respondents who wanted to leave were asked whether they would still consider moving if the neighborhood were all white.

A final question intended to gauge racial attitudes asked for suggestions about how the neighborhood could be improved. This question served as a reliability check in that the content of the response sometimes tended to confirm or to contradict responses which appeared elsewhere in the questionnaire.

Interview procedure.—Interviewers were instructed to exercise judgment and to withdraw from any situation if they felt respondents were apprehensive or antagonistic with respect to any aspect of the interview. Several respondents demanded to see credentials which each interviewer carried, but only a few people telephoned the University to inquire about the study. Space on the front of the questionnaire for address of the property and similar information was deliberately left blank until after the interview was completed and the interviewer left the house. No names were entered on questionnaires and respondents were assured that the information would be used only in statistical form. Interviewers called back once at each property on their first tour of the neighborhood. Second and third call-backs were usually made in the evening or on weekends. Three call-backs were standard procedure and properties that were in a neighborhood where field work was still in process were revisited as many as four and five times. Very few respondents failed to be contacted and there were virtually no refusals.

SURVEY OF INFORMED PERSONS

An additional survey was made of informed persons in order to explore the possible interrelationships between racial change and neighborhood life as seen by individuals and organizations concerned with specific aspects of community affairs. Interviews with four city-wide agencies provided a list of potential respondents from which twenty were chosen at random. The list included church, business, real estate, and school personnel, as well as leaders of social agencies and civic organizations.

An unstructured personal interview was employed with specific interview guides prepared for each respondent. If the respondent did not mention racial change in describing his activity, the interviewer did so. All interviews were conducted by the same staff member and took from one to three hours each. This was followed by a mail-back questionnaire which dealt with population patterns and trends and which was identical for all respondents.

THE PURCHASER QUESTIONNAIRE

UNIVERSITY OF PENNSYLVANIA, INSTITUTE FOR URBAN STUDIES

HOUSING AND NEIGHBORHOOD STUDY

TO BE CHECKED BY INTERVIEWER

1. Area .... 2. Census tract .... 3. Block ....

4. Address .... 5. Date ....

6. Schedule No. .... 7. Total time consumed ....
(no. of minutes)

8. Interviewer ....

   I'm from the University of Pennsylvania. We are making a study of neighborhoods and housing and we would like to ask you a few questions about your neighborhood and household. It won't take more than about ten minutes.

   First of all, I'd like to talk over the way you and your family feel about your present home and how you happen to live here.

1. When did you move to this house? ....
(month and year)

2. How long have you lived in this neighborhood? ....
(no. of years)

3. How did you learn that this house was for sale? ....
   ....
   ....

4. Where did you live before moving to this neighborhood? *(Philadelphia metropolitan area address, or if respondent lived on a farm get town and city and state).*

   ....
(exact address)

5. *(If previous residence was Philadelphia metropolitan area)* How long have you lived in the Philadelphia area? ....
(no. of years)

6. When you decided to move from your last home, in which other areas did you look for a place to live? ....
(*If respondent looked only in this area OMIT questions 7 and 8*)

Comments: ....
....
....

7. Which of these areas did you want to move into as a first choice, second choice, etc.? ....
(*Be sure to get all areas which the respondent prefers to his present neighborhood*).

8. Perhaps you can tell me why you decided to move into this area instead of (*here use name of area that respondent gave as first choice*).
(*If questions 7 and 8 are answered OMIT 9 and go to 10*).

9. Can you tell me the reasons why this area was given first choice? ....

10. Did you find out anything which caused you to doubt your choice of house or neighborhood, before you moved here? Yes .... No ....

11. (*If answer to question 10 is yes*) What were these doubts?
....

12. Now that you have lived here for a while, are you in any way dissatisfied with your home? Yes .... No ....
Your neighborhood? Yes .... No ....

13. (*If answer to question 12 is yes*) What makes you feel dissatisfied? ....
What dissatisfied you most? ....

(*If Negroes have not been mentioned up to this point, ask question 14. If Negroes have been mentioned, OMIT questions 14 and 15*).

14. Are there any people in the neighborhood whose race or reli-

gion is different from yours? Yes .... No ....
Don't know ....

15. (*If answer to question 14 is yes*) Who are they? ....
....

*If respondent HAS mentioned Negroes up to this point, go on to
page 3 and then on to page 4.*
*If respondent HAS NOT mentioned Negroes up to this point,
omit page 3 and go directly to page 4.*
Comments: ....
....
....
....
....
....

(*Use this page only if respondent has mentioned Negroes previously*).

16. When did you find out that Negroes live in this neighborhood
    —before or after you decided to buy this house? ....
    ....

17. How do you feel about owning a house—
    In the same neighborhood with Negroes? ....
    On the same block? ....
    Next door? ....

(*Probe to see if respondent distinguishes between row house,
semi-detached and free standing single family house*).

18. Do you want to leave this neighborhood or would you like
    to stay here?
    Wants to leave .... Wants to stay .... Undecided ....
    Check one and write in whatever respondent says ....
    ....

19. (*To be asked of those respondents who want to leave or are
    undecided*) Are you actively looking for another place to
    live? ....
    ....

20. (*To be asked of those respondents who want to leave*) If the families living in this neighborhood were all white, would you still want to leave the neighborhood? Yes .... No .... Why is that? ....

Comments: ....
....
....
....
....

I have just a few more questions to ask you.

21. (*Circle respondent, no names, estimate ages of adults, get ages of children*).
    Who else lives here?

Relationship	Sex	Age
1.		
2.		
3.		
4.		
5.		
6.		

22. What State (or foreign country if not USA) were
    (a) you born in? ....
    (b) your husband (wife)? ....

23. Where were your parents born? ....
    your husband's (wife's parents)? ....

24. What does the head of the house do for a living? (*Get specific answer*) ....

25. Where is his place of work located? (*Exact address or street intersections, if no specific place of employment get usual area of operation*) ....
    ....

26. Does anyone else in the household work full time? Yes............
    No .... (*List relationships*) ....

27. Are your monthly payments
    Less than $40
    between $40 and $59
    between $60 and $79
    between $80 and $99
    $100 and over (*Circle appropriate interval*)

    (*If there is a strong objection to question 27 OMIT 28*)

28. Was your total family income in 1955—
    less than $4,000
    between $4,000 and $5,900
    between $6,000 and $7,900
    between $8,000 and $9,900
    Over $10,000 (*Circle appropriate interval*)

29. What is your religious preference? ....
    your husband's (wife's)? ....

30. Are you (is your husband) a veteran? Yes .... No ....

31. How many years of school did you finish? (*Write in whatever
    the respondent says*) ....

32. Do you have any suggestions about how the neighborhood
    could be improved? ....

Statistical Tables

TABLE D-1

POPULATION BY RACE, CITY OF PHILADELPHIA, 1850–1950

Year	Population			Nonwhite population as a percent of total
	White	Nonwhite[a]	Total	
1850	389,001	19,761	408,762	4.8
1860	543,344	22,185	565,529	3.9
1870	651,875	22,147	674,022	3.3
1880	815,471	31,699	847,170	3.7
1890	1,007,593	39,371	1,046,964	3.7
1900	1,229,673	64,024	1,293,697	4.9
1910	1,463,371	85,637	1,549,008	5.5
1920	1,688,180	135,599	1,823,779	7.4
1930	1,728,457	222,504	1,950,961	11.4
1940	1,678,577	252,757	1,931,334	13.1
1950	1,692,637	378,968	2,071,605	18.3

SOURCE: U. S. Bureau of the Census. Reprinted in I. Maximilian Martin, *Housing Problems of the Philadelphia Nonwhite Population* (Philadelphia: Isadore Martin, 1953), table 1, p. 3, and *Philadelphia's Negro Population, Facts on Housing* (City of Philadelphia, Commission on Human Relations, October, 1953), table 1, p. 5.

[a]Figures for years 1850 through 1890 refer to Negroes only. From 1900 to 1950 the number of nonwhites other than Negroes increased from approximately 1,400 to 2,900.

TABLE D-2

CHANGES IN THE POPULATION, BY RACE, FOR INTERCENSAL DECADES,
CITY OF PHILADELPHIA, 1850–1950

Intercensal decade	Change in white population		Change in nonwhite population		Change in total population	
	Number	Percent	Number	Percent	Number	Percent
1850–1860	154,343	39.7	2,424	12.3	156,767	38.4
1860–1870	108,531	20.0	–38	–0.2	108,493	19.2
1870–1880	163,596	25.1	9,552	43.1	173,148	25.7
1880–1890	192,122	23.6	7,672	24.2	199,794	23.6
1890–1900	222,080	22.0	24,653	38.5	246,733	23.6
1900–1910	233,698	19.0	21,613	33.8	255,311	19.7
1910–1920	224,809	15.4	49,962	58.3	274,771	17.7
1920–1930	40,277	2.4	86,905	64.0	127,182	7.0
1930–1940	–49,880	–2.9	30,253	13.6	–19,627	–1.0
1940–1950	14,060	0.8	126,211	49.9	140,271	7.3

SOURCE: Table D-1.

TABLE D-3

NUMBER OF NEGRO-OCCUPIED HOMES AND NEGRO HOMEOWNERS,
CITY OF PHILADELPHIA, 1900–1956

Year	Negro homes	Negro homeowners	Negro homeownership rate (percent)
1900	12,200	516	4
1910	18,095	905	5
1920	30,995	3,778	12
1930	50,997	7,830	15
1940	65,492	6,600	10
1950	99,881	29,149	29
1956	126,371	55,411	44

SOURCE: Figures for 1900 to 1950 are from U. S. Census data. They appear in I. Maximilian Martin, *Housing Problems of the Philadelphia Nonwhite Population* (Philadelphia: Isadore Martin, 1953), table 3, p. 13. Figures for 1956 are from unpublished data of the U. S. Bureau of the Census, *1956 National Housing Inventory*, Philadelphia Supplement.

TABLE D-4

CHARACTERISTICS OF STUDY AREAS

Characteristic	West Phila-delphia	Strawberry Mansion	Tasker	Old City
Number of blocks, 1950	414	229	219	114
Number of blocks with dwelling units, 1950	404	219	188	71
Number of occupied dwelling units, 1950	24,712	12,112	8,632	1,885
Dwelling units occupied by nonwhites, 1950				
Number	523	2,684	2,395	345
Percent	2.1	22.2	27.8	18.3
Dwelling units lacking private bath or dilapidated, 1950				
Number	600	1,314	609	454
Percent	2.5	10.8	7.2	24.1
Dwelling units lacking running water or dilapidated, 1950				
Number	286	445	396	137
Percent	1.2	3.7	4.7	7.3

TABLE D-5

BONA FIDE TRANSFERS OF SINGLE FAMILY HOMES,
FOUR STUDY AREAS, 1955

Area	Transfers			
	White	Negro	Absentee	Total
West Philadelphia	286	864	132	1,282
Strawberry Mansion	25	640	131	796
Tasker	128	70	58	256
Old City	4	. . .	2	6
All Areas	443	1,574	323	2,340

TABLE D-6

Percent Distribution of Households by Presence of Children under 18 Years, White and Negro Purchasers and White Renters in the Study Areas, 1955

| | White purchasers | | | | | | | | Negro purchasers | | White renters | |
| | West Phila. | | Straw. Mans. | | Tasker | | All areas[a] | | All areas[a] | | West Phila. | |
	Number	Percent	Number	Percent	Number	Percent	Number	Percent	Number	Percent	Number	Percent
Households without children	39	31.0	5	35.7	9	16.7	53	27.3	79	40.3	61	61.0
Households with children	87	69.0	9	64.3	45	83.3	141	72.7	117	59.7	39	39.0
Households with school age children	57	45.2	7	50.0	31	57.4	95	49.0	87	44.4	19	19.0
Households with pre-school children only	30	23.8	2	14.3	14	25.9	46	23.7	30	15.3	20	20.0
Total	126	100.0	14	100.0	54	100.0	194	100.0	196	100.0	100	100.0

[a] Refers to the three study areas from which the samples were drawn: West Philadelphia, Strawberry Mansion and Tasker. This applies to every table employing the column heading "All areas" for White or Negro purchasers.

TABLE D-7

PERCENT DISTRIBUTION OF HOUSEHOLDS BY NUMBER OF SCHOOL AGE CHILDREN, WHITE AND NEGRO PURCHASERS AND WHITE RENTERS IN THE STUDY AREAS, 1955

| Number of school age children | White purchasers | | | | | | | | Negro purchasers | | White renters | |
| | West Phila. | | Straw. Mans. | | Tasker | | All areas[a] | | All areas[a] | | West Phila. | |
	Number	Percent	Number	Percent	Number	Percent	Number	Percent	Number	Percent	Number	Percent
0	69	54.8	7	50.0	23	42.6	99	51.0	109	55.6	81	81.0
1	28	22.1	6	42.9	18	33.2	52	26.9	42	21.4	12	12.0
2	22	17.5	1	7.1	6	11.1	29	14.9	22	11.2	1	1.0
3 or more	7	5.6	....	....	7	13.1	14	7.2	23	11.8	6	6.0
Total	126	100.0	14	100.0	54	100.0	194	100.0	196	100.0	100	100.0

[a]See footnote a, table D-6.

TABLE D-8

PERCENT DISTRIBUTION OF HOUSEHOLDS BY FAMILY COMPOSITION, WHITE AND NEGRO PURCHASERS AND WHITE RENTERS IN THE STUDY AREAS, 1955

| Family composition | White purchasers | | | | | | | | Negro purchasers | | White renters | |
| | West Phila. | | Straw. Mans. | | Tasker | | All areas[a] | | All areas[a] | | West Phila. | |
	Number	Percent	Number	Percent	Number	Percent	Number	Percent	Number	Percent	Number	Percent
Husband and wife	107	84.9	12	85.7	52	96.3	171	88.1	168	85.7	71	71.0
Other families	16	12.7	2	14.3	2	3.7	20	10.3	17	8.7	7	7.0
Unrelated persons	3	2.4	....	....	....	....	3	1.6	11	5.6	22	22.0
Total	126	100.0	14	100.0	54	100.0	194	100.0	196	100.0	100	100.0

[a]See footnote a, table D-6.

TABLE D-9

PERCENT DISTRIBUTION OF HOUSEHOLDS BY AGE OF HOUSEHOLD HEAD,
WHITE AND NEGRO PURCHASERS AND WHITE RENTERS IN THE
STUDY AREAS, 1955

Age of head of household	White purchasers				Negro purchasers	White renters
	W. Phila.	Straw. Man.	Tasker	All areas[a]	All areas[a]	W. Phila.
Under 30	20.6	7.1	33.3	23.2	27.0	33.0
30–39	34.9	42.9	37.0	36.1	41.8	21.0
40–49	18.3	7.1	14.8	16.5	16.8	16.0
50–64	12.7	7.1	13.0	12.4	11.2	20.0
65 and over	7.9	28.6	1.9	7.7	1.6	9.0
No answer	5.6	7.1	. . .	4.1	1.6	1.0
Total	100.0	100.0	100.0	100.0	100.0	100.0
Median Age (years)	37	38	35	36	34	37

[a] See footnote a, table D-6.

TABLE D-10

Percent Distribution of Households by Years of School Completed by Household Head, White Purchasers and White Renters in the Study Areas, 1955

| Years of school completed | White Purchasers | | | | White renters West Phila. |
	West Phila.	Straw. Mans.	Tasker	All areas[a]	
Less than 8	11.9	35.7	14.8	14.5	5.0
8 to 11	46.0	50.0	48.1	46.9	40.0
12	30.2	7.2	33.3	29.4	29.0
College (1 or more years)	9.5	...	3.7	7.2	14.0
Other (beyond high school)	1.6	...	...	1.0	5.0
No answer	0.8	7.2	...	1.0	7.0
Total	100.0	100.0	100.0	100.0	100.0
Median number of years of school completed	10	9	10	10	12
	White / Negro	White / Negro	White / Negro	White / Negro	White / Negro
Median number of years of school completed by *all* residents over 25 years of age, by race, 1950[b]	11.3 / 8.8	8.6 / 8.3	8.5 / 7.9	... / ...	11.3 / 8.8

[a] See footnote a, table D-6.
[b] U. S. Census of Population: 1950, vol. III, *Census Tract Statistics*, chap. 42, "Philadelphia."

TABLE D-11

PERCENT DISTRIBUTION OF HOUSEHOLDS BY OCCUPATION OF HOUSEHOLD HEAD, WHITE
AND NEGRO PURCHASERS AND WHITE RENTERS IN THE STUDY AREAS, 1955

Occupation	White purchasers				Negro purchasers	White renters
	W. Phila.	Straw. Man.	Tasker	All areas[a]	All areas[a]	W. Phila.
Professional	10.4	. . .	3.7	7.8	6.1	17.1
Proprietor and manager	8.8	14.0	3.7	7.8	3.1	3.1
Clerical	9.6	7.0	7.4	9.0	10.7	15.1
Sales	4.1	7.0	9.3	5.8	2.0	12.1
Craftsmen and foremen	30.3	7.0	29.5	28.7	19.4	11.1
Operatives	17.6	35.0	22.2	20.3	25.0	9.1
Service workers	8.8	14.0	7.4	9.0	13.8	6.1
Laborers	1.6	. . .	13.0	4.7	13.3	2.0
Others	1.6	. . .	1.9	1.6	0.5	8.1
Retired	5.7	14.0	1.9	5.3	1.0	12.1
No answer and don't know	1.5	2.0	. . .	. . .	5.0	4.1
Total	100.0	100.0	100.0	100.0	100.0	100.0

[a]See footnote a, table D-6.

TABLE D-12

PERCENT DISTRIBUTION OF HOUSEHOLDS BY PRESENCE OF SECONDARY WORKER, WHITE
AND NEGRO PURCHASERS AND WHITE RENTERS IN THE STUDY AREAS, 1955

Presence of secondary full-time worker	White purchasers				Negro purchasers	White renters
	W. Phila.	Straw. Man.	Tasker	All areas[a]	All areas[a]	W. Phila.
Yes	31.7	7.1	26.0	28.4	46.9	32.0
No	65.9	85.8	74.0	69.6	48.5	56.0
No answer	2.4	7.1	. . .	2.0	4.6	12.0
Total	100.0	100.0	100.0	100.0	100.0	100.0

[a]See footnote a, table D-6.

TABLE D-13

PERCENT DISTRIBUTION OF HOUSEHOLDS BY TOTAL INCOME OF HOUSEHOLD, WHITE
AND NEGRO PURCHASERS AND WHITE RENTERS IN THE STUDY AREAS, 1955

Income	White purchasers				Negro purchasers	White renters
	W. Phila.	Straw. Man.	Tasker	All areas[a]	All areas[a]	W. Phila.
Less than $4,000	14.3	28.6	31.5	20.1	17.3	36.0
$4,000 to $5,999	46.8	14.3	44.4	43.8	40.8	28.0
$6,000 to $7,999	15.1	14.3	5.5	12.4	9.2	11.0
$8,000 to $9,999	. . .	. . .	2.0	.5	1.0	1.0
$10,000 and over	.8	. . .	. . .	.5	. . .	2.0
No answer and don't know	23.0	42.8	16.6	22.7	31.7	22.0
Total	100.0	100.0	100.0	100.0	100.0	100.0
Median income	$5,050	$4,000	$4,460	$4,850	$4,830	$4,210

[a] See footnote a, table D-6.

TABLE D-14

PERCENT DISTRIBUTION OF HEADS OF HOUSEHOLDS AND WIVES BY PLACE OF BIRTH,
WHITE PURCHASERS AND RENTERS IN THE STUDY AREAS, 1955

Place of birth	White purchasers								White renters West Phila.	
	West Phila.		Straw. Man.		Tasker		All areas			
	Head	Wife	Head	Wife	Head	Wife	Head	Wife	Head	Wife
North Atlantic States	67.5	72.0	57.2	50.0	83.3	90.4	71.2	76.0	74.0	. . .
Other sections of the U. S.	12.7	13.0	7.1	. . .	3.7	3.8	9.8	9.2	11.0	. . .
Eastern Europe	8.7	5.6	28.6	33.4	. . .	. . .	7.7	5.9	7.0	. . .
Other sections of Europe	10.3	4.7	. . .	. . .	11.1	5.8	9.8	4.8	3.0	. . .
Elsewhere	. . .	. . .	7.1	8.3	1.9	. . .	1.0	0.6	. . .	. . .
No answer	0.8	4.7	. . .	8.3	. . .	. . .	.5	3.5	5.0	. . .
Total	100.0	100.0	100.0	100.0	100.0	100.0	100.0	100.0	100.0	

TABLE D-15

PERCENT DISTRIBUTION OF PARENTS OF HEADS OF HOUSEHOLDS AND WIVES BY PLACE OF
BIRTH, WHITE PURCHASERS AND RENTERS IN THE STUDY AREAS, 1955

Place of birth of parents	White purchasers								White renters West Phila.	
	West Phila.		Straw. Man.		Tasker		All areas[a]			
	Head	Wife	Head	Wife	Head	Wife	Head	Wife	Head	Wife[a]
Both U. S.	50.0	50.2	35.7	8.3	50.0	90.4	48.9	59.6	55.0	...
At least one East Europe	16.6	11.8	57.2	50.0	3.7	3.8	16.0	12.3	22.0	...
At least one Italy	8.7	4.5	...	8.3	25.8	...	12.9	3.5	2.0	...
At least one Ireland	15.9	12.8	...	...	7.4	5.8	12.4	9.9	6.0	...
Other European	4.0	6.3	...	8.3	9.3	...	5.2	5.1	5.0	...
Elsewhere	...	6.3	...	8.3	1.9	...	.5	3.2	2.0	...
No answer and not known	4.8	8.1	7.1	16.8	1.9	...	4.1	6.4	8.0	...
Total	100.0	100.0	100.0	100.0	100.0	100.0	100.0	100.0	100.0	

[a] See footnote a, table D-6.
[a] For white renters, data are available only for the parents of the household head.

TABLE D-16

PERCENT DISTRIBUTION OF HOUSEHOLDS BY RELIGIOUS PREFERENCE OF HEAD OF
HOUSEHOLD, WHITE PURCHASERS AND RENTERS IN STUDY AREAS, 1955

Religious preference	White purchasers				White renters West Phila.
	West Phila.	Straw. Mans.	Tasker	All areas	
Catholic	65.1	28.6	83.3	67.5	35.0
Protestant	22.2	14.3	16.7	20.1	45.0
Jewish	11.1	57.1	...	11.3	14.0
No answer	1.6	...	...	1.1	6.0
Total	100.0	100.0	100.0	100.0	100.0

TABLE D-17

SOURCES OF FUNDS FOR HOME PURCHASES BY RACE
AND TYPE OF PURCHASER, ALL STUDY AREAS, 1955

Source of funds	Owner-occupants				Absentee		Total purchases	
	White		Negro					
	No.	Pct.	No.	Pct.	No.	Pct.	No.	Pct.
New or refinanced mortgages								
Institutional	361	82.4	1,500	95.2	189	58.8	2,050	87.8
Individual purchase-money mortgages	8	1.8	19	1.2	7	2.2	34	1.5
Other individual mortgages	21	4.8	26	1.7	35	10.9	82	3.5
Miscellaneous sources[a]	3	0.7	14	0.9	4	1.2	21	0.9
Total	393	89.7	1,559	99.0	235	73.1	2,187	93.7
Subject mortgages	3	0.7	7	0.4	26	8.1	36	1.5
All mortgages	396	90.4	1,566	99.4	261	81.2	2,223	95.2
Full cash payment without mortgages	42	9.6	9	0.6	60	18.7	111	4.8
Grand total	438	100.0	1,575	100.0	321	100.0	2,334	100.0

[a]Includes such sources as clubs, benevolent associations, etc.

TABLE D-18

SOURCE OF MORTGAGE FUNDS FOR THE PURCHASE OF SINGLE-FAMILY HOMES
BY RACE AND TYPE OF PURCHASER AND TYPE OF LENDING INSTITUTION,
ALL STUDY AREAS, 1955

Type of lending institution	Owner-occupant purchases				Absentee purchases		Total purchases	
	White		Negro					
	No.	Pct.	No.	Pct.	No.	Pct.	No.	Pct.
Savings and loan associations								
Federal	114	26.0	659	41.8	72	22.4	845	36.2
State	113	25.8	485	30.8	74	23.1	672	28.8
Mutual savings banks	43	9.8	107	6.8	3	0.9	153	6.5
Banking and trust companies	17	3.9	24	1.5	3	0.9	44	1.9
Insurance companies	12	2.7	19	1.2	28	8.7	59	2.5
Mortgage service companies	62	14.2	206	13.1	9	2.8	277	11.9
Subtotal[a]	361	82.4	1,500	95.2	189	58.8	2,050	87.8
All other sources	77	17.6	75	4.8	132	41.2	284	12.2
Grand total	438	100.0	1,575	100.0	321	100.0	2,334	100.0

[a]Includes one purchase financed with a purchase-money mortgage.

TABLE D-19

NUMBER AND TYPES OF INSTITUTIONS THAT FINANCED HOME PURCHASES
IN THE FOUR STUDY AREAS, 1955

Type of institution	Number of institutions making mortgage loans in the study areas	Total number of loans made	Average number of loans per institution
Savings and loan associations	101	1,517	15
Mutual savings banks	3	153	51
Banking and trust companies	7	44	6
Mortgage companies	14	277	20
Life insurance companies	5	59	12
Other institutions	5	9	2
Total	135	2,059	

TABLE D-20

SALES PRICE OF 1955 HOME PURCHASES BY RACE
AND TYPE OF PURCHASER, ALL STUDY AREAS

Sales price	Owner-occupant				Absentee		Total	
	White		Nonwhite					
	No.	Pct.	No.	Pct.	No.	Pct.	No.	Pct.
Under $5,000	60	13.7	104	6.6	157	48.9	321	13.8
$5,000–$5,999	62	14.2	270	17.1	42	13.1	374	16.0
$6,000–$6,999	76	17.4	292	18.5	37	11.5	405	17.3
$7,000–$7,999	71	16.2	380	24.1	33	10.3	484	20.7
$8,000–$8,999	65	14.8	258	16.4	22	6.9	345	14.8
$9,000–$9,999	42	9.6	118	7.5	8	2.5	168	7.2
$10,000–$10,999	32	7.3	77	4.9	13	4.0	122	5.2
$11,000–$11,999	14	3.2	42	2.7	6	1.9	62	2.7
$12,000 and over	16	3.6	34	2.2	3	.9	53	2.3
Total	438	100.0	1,575	100.0	321	100.0	2,334	100.0
Total amount (dollars)	3,216,000		11,563,000		1,722,000		16,501,000	
Mean sales price (dollars)	7,345		7,340		5,365		7,070	
Median sales price (dollars)	7,295		7,320		5,070		7,140	

TABLE D-21

RELATIONSHIP OF MORTGAGE LOAN–SALES PRICE RATIOS TO SALES PRICE,
AND SALES PRICE–ASSESSED VALUE RATIOS, WHITE AND NEGRO PURCHASES,
MIXED SECTION, WEST PHILADELPHIA STUDY AREA, 1955

Ratio of mortgage loan to sales price	Percent of purchases by—		Mean purchase price for—		Mean SP–AV ratio for—	
	White buyers	Negro buyers	White buyers	Negro buyers	White buyers	Negro buyers
.90 to 1.00	40	60	$7,445	$8,310	1.85	1.86
.80 to .89	8	20	8,275	8,420	1.71	1.83
Below .80	38	19	7,775	9,120	1.72	1.87
No mortgage	14	1	7,745	7,520	1.63	1.67
Total[a]	100	100	$7,680	$8,310	1.75	1.85

[a]There were 863 sales to Negroes and 99 sales to whites.

Index